DESERT IMAGES

An American Landscape

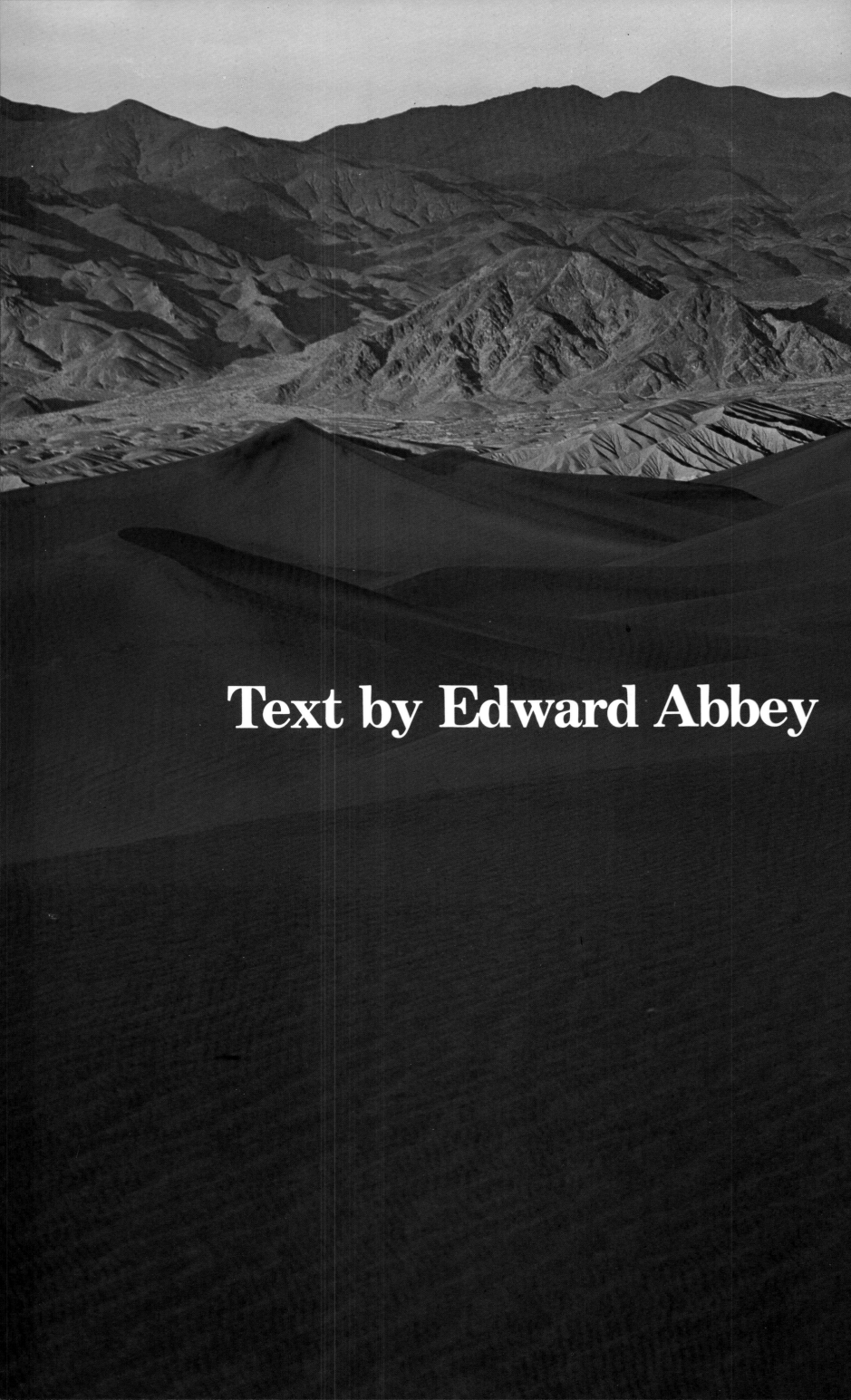

Text by Edward Abbey

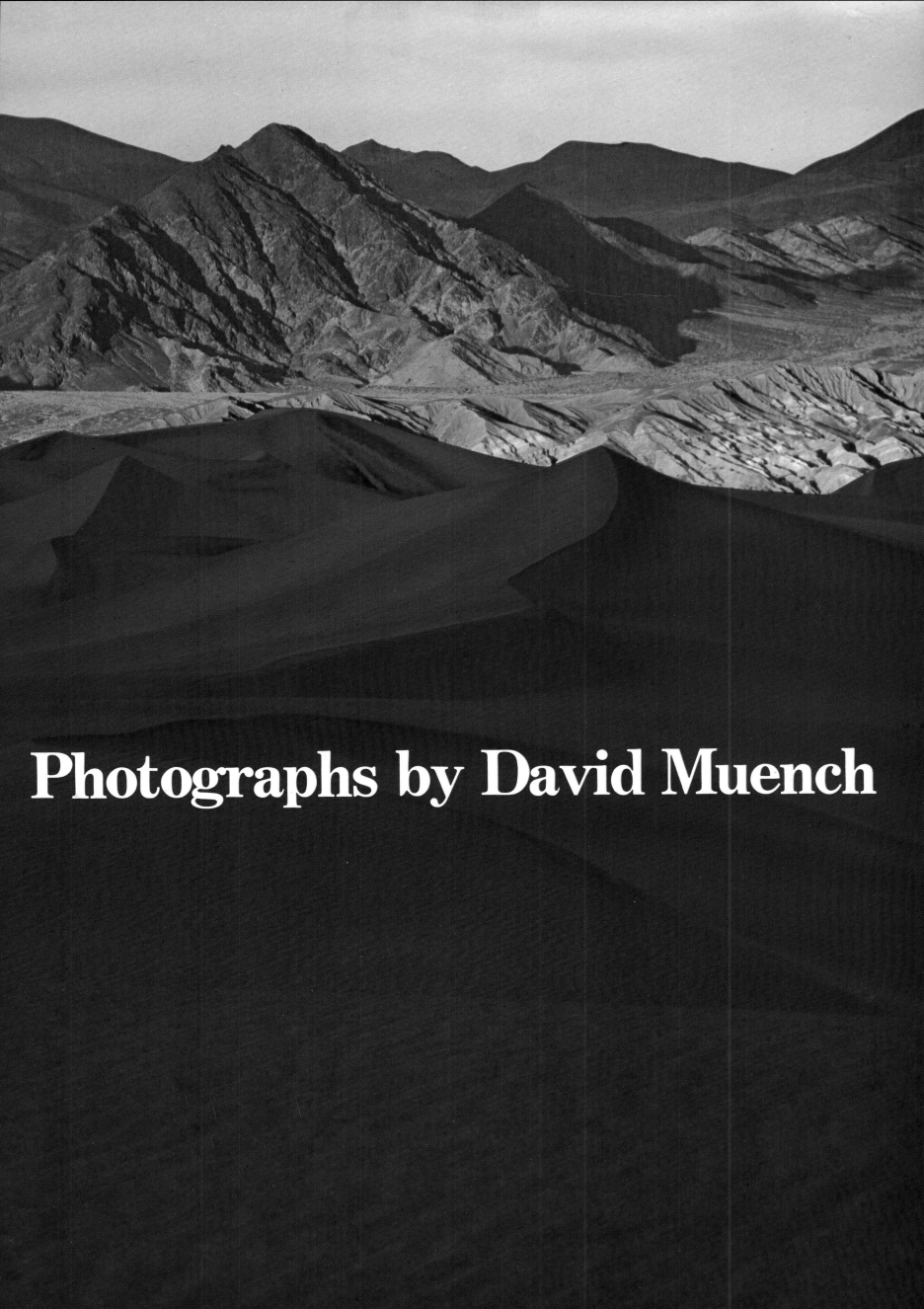

Photographs by David Muench

Picture Editor, Susan Rayfield   Design and Coordination by Massimo Vignelli and Gudrun Buettner

A Chanticleer Press Edition · Gallery Books · W. H. Smith Publishers, Inc. · New York

Death Valley transformations:
Sand dunes of Mesquite Flat
in foreground, Grapevine
Mountains beyond, seen from
the west at different times
of day.
First Frontispiece:
Sunrise 7:15 a.m.
Second Frontispiece:
Midafternoon 2:30 p.m.
Third Frontispiece:
Nightfall 6:00 p.m.
Fourth Frontispiece:
Evening 6:30 p.m.

Photograph of Edward Abbey by Michael Hendrickson
Photograph of David Muench by David Muench

Requests for permission to make copies of any part of the work should be mailed to: Gallery Books, W. H. Smith Publishers, Inc., 112 Madison Avenue, New York, New York 10016.

Printed and bound by Dai Nippon, Tokyo, Japan.

Library of Congress Cataloging in Publication Data
Muench, David
Desert images.
1. Photography, Artistic.   2. Deserts—United States.   I. Abbey, Edward, 1927-   II. Title.
TR654.M83   779'.9'978   78-4889
ISBN 0-8317-2189-8

First edition, 1979, published by Harcourt Brace Jovanovich, New York.

Third printing, 1987, by Gallery Books, an imprint of W.H. Smith Publishers, Inc.

Contents

Something wakes her before dawn. An odd sound, unexpected in this lonely place, as of human voices. Intimate voices from a remote time, speaking a language that is not her own but much older. Voices without words, a confused but liquid murmur, soft, gentle, far away. Far below. Puzzled for a moment, she raises her head from the sleeping bag and listens. She notices that the wind has changed direction, bringing up to her what she could not hear last night—the voice of the river. The talk of many waters, marvelously complex, sliding past sandbars, pouring to the drop-off, clashing with one another in turmoil and frenzy (but in a luxury of surrender, the ease of joy, yielding without pain or resistance to the greater force, bound once again for the circle of the sea, the call of the winds that encircle the planet). The voice of the desert.

Glittering Orion hangs overhead, but on the east, above the dark flat bulk of the plateau, a plane of silver and pale green lies across the horizon. She opens her warm cocoon, dresses quickly, shivering in the chill air, builds a little fire of juniper twigs on the cold sand, heats water for tea. Waiting, she walks to the edge of the rimrock and peers down, downward, three thousand vertical feet, to the starlit river. A thread of bright metal winding among cliffs, down in the rich darkness of the canyon, speaking to her, to the sleeping herons in the willow trees. A few days earlier she had been down there, in a small boat, plunging through the roar of the rapids, a sound transmuted now, into nonhuman but comforting voices. The river is the heart of the desert. She is a lover of that river, and of the great canyon that the river has created, and of the desert that surrounds her.

Back to her little fire. She drinks hot tea from a tin cup, eats cold cereal from a warm bowl, and watches the approach of morning. In the clear dry air of the desert the transition from night to day is brief compared to that of more humid and human climates, but equally beautiful. Finishing her breakfast she takes the cased flute from her pack, assembles its three parts, warms it in her hands, and waits for the rise of the sun. The stars are fading. Spokes of light probe through fiery clouds on the east, illuminate the crest of the plateau, light up the cliffs around her with a tangerine glow. From the shadows far below come the first tentative bird cries, mingling with, then rising above the remote but intimate voice of the river.

Introduction:

Responding to the birds, she plays a few high notes on the flute, stops and listens to the resonance of the stillness. Her little phrase comes back, after a while, from the distant walls of the plateau. She plays the tune again, her morning song, urging the sun upward. Again she stops and listens to that silence which surrounds all song and makes it more poignant and beautiful than music, in itself, can be.

The echoes come back, transformed by the immense distance, reshaped by the currents of the air. She plays the song a third time and stops. The silence that follows is broken by the cry of a coyote on the plateau, a barbaric yawping carried from rim to rim, across the canyon, over the buttes and mesas and pinnacles of stone that rise from shadows into sunlight. A song of the self, of hunger, of loneliness hungering for an end to loneliness. A song of the desert.

The sun bulges above the horizon, warped by time and the prisms of the sky. Resurrection. It bulges with power, dripping flames, glaring through its own distortions. The desert rolls toward the sun, the sun breaks clear of the skyline and floats on a sea of green beyond shoals of clouds with hard and gilded edges, vermilion depths. An armada of clouds sailing out of nowhere into nothingness. The woman stands and plays her flute, facing the sun, helping that old star clear the sky, helping the earth roll on toward it. The light streams across league after league of redrock wilderness—the Painted Desert, Echo Cliffs, Cape Solitude—and onto the walls, cliffs, terraces and towers of Marble Gorge, Tonto Rim, Conquistador Aisle, dispelling the purple shadows of the master canyon. Out of the unknown into mystery. The light of the desert.

The flutist concludes her sunrise music, puts the gleaming instrument away, shoulders her pack, and continues the walk she had begun three days before. She follows a deer path that winds among boulders, junipers, clumps of cactus, cliff rose, the tall, infinitely lovely seedstalks of a desert lily. She has only about ten miles to go before she reaches the road, a dusty car, the way that will take her home again. And where is home? She doesn't care. For one whose senses and emotions are alive, home is anywhere—and everywhere. She is at ease in the arid wasteland where nothing human can find permanent habitation and in the roaring canyons of the city filled with people who spend their entire lives in rooms and streets. All deserts begin in the mind.

13

On the Canyon Rim

We fly above it all. Altitude 7,500 feet, air speed 140 knots, course 3.20, bound for Las Vegas, Nevada from Moab, Utah. Two of us in a Cessna 182, me the helpless passenger and my friend T. K. Arnold the pilot. He is reading *Playboy*, I hold the controls. I'm driving. A single white cloud sails rapidly toward us; I pull back on the yoke, pull up the nose. We fly into the cloud and all becomes opaque and white, a world of vapor without sign of orientation. "Watch your instruments," says Arnold, not glancing up from his magazine.

We fly through the cloud into the clear. The Green River meanders beneath us, a narrow strip of golden water and green tamarisk winding in loops and bowknots through the burnt orange, pale lemon, and manganese oxides of the sandstone bedrock. Shapes out of fantasy, out of surrealistic dreams, pass below: goblins and hobgoblins, domes and spires, grottos, alcoves, amphitheaters, abandoned cities of stone half-buried in sand, long reptilian ridges like melted dragons. . . . The canyons divide and subdivide, taper off under overhanging ledges, each of which provides a spectacular waterfall when it rains. If it rains.

Beyond the river we pass over the Green River Desert, a fifty-mile-wide expanse of red earth and coral-colored sand dunes. The dunes, all crescent-shaped from the prevailing winds, resemble the serried scallops of a cabbage shredder. The desert is crossed and scored with long thin lines, old Jeep and truck roads left by the oil and uranium prospectors, but no one lives down there. No one but the lizards, the mice, a few birds, rabbits, coyotes, snakes. This land reminds me of the red heart, the dead heart (as they call it) of Australia. But of course the desert is not dead. Sparsely inhabited, yes, unfit for humans, certainly, but by no means dead. Given a little rain in the right amounts, at the right time, and that arid, seared desolation below will be carpeted, briefly but gloriously, with sunflowers, globe mallows, primroses, verbena, asters, dozens of others. With or without those transient flowers the Green River Desert is beautiful. The little animals like it. The vultures like it. The scorpions like it. And I like it.

Arnold turns a page. I drive our little airplane above the Dirty Devil River and the wrinkled clay hills near Hanksville (population 275, counting dogs—commercial and cultural hub of south-central Utah).

14

From the Eagle's View

The Henry Mountains loom on our left, an isolated laccolithic range with peaks up to 11,000 feet high, covered with pine, scrub oak, pinyon pine, juniper, but spawning no streams. Dry mountains, an island of dry forest surrounded by deserts of stone, sand, clay, the burnt-out, dried-up, over-grazed wasteland. Beautiful!

From the air one can see most clearly the pattern of the desert. Each drainage channel eats into the hills in perfect arboreal fashion, the main channel forming the trunk, its tributaries the limbs, each limb in turn equipped with its set of branches, twigs, stems, the veins of leaves.

Approaching Capitol Reef, the Waterpocket Fold, Boulder Mountain and the high plateaus beyond—Aquarius, Fishlake, Paunsagunt— Arnold says, "Take her up to ten." I pull up the nose, the plane slowing, engine laboring, as we climb the mountains of the air. We cross the reef at 9,500. Another wonderland of buff-colored sandstone, an intricate labyrinth of deep, dark, narrow canyons carved by a million years of storm and weathering from the flanks of a great monocline a hundred miles long. Beyond are the Circle Cliffs, forty or fifty miles of watermelon-colored sandstone walls partly enclosing a wild and lovely tableland known as the Purple Hills country. Wild—but threatened. The power industry is training its cyclops eye on this place, searching for oil, gas, coal, uranium, potash, anything saleable.

A trifle. All such annoyances will pass, give or take another century or two. If enlightenment fails we have, as always, the traditional solution—disaster—to fall back upon. Upward and onward with the arts. Our tiny tin bird wobbles, bumps, bounces, over the moguls in the air, propeller dragging us onward. Forests pass below, dense stands of yellow pine, spruce, fir, aspen. Small lakes wink in the sunlight, fields of snow cover the mountain meadows. Still winter down there.

We fly over the peppermint-candy rock of Bryce Canyon National Park, then above a high, bleak, gray-green mountain valley and past the mighty towers of Zion. Angel's Landing lies below. The narrow gorge of the Virgin River. The rosy escarpments of the Kolob Canyons. The small city of St. George, Utah's Dixie, where Brigham Young (that old ram, patriarch, reincarnation of Moses, Abraham and Isaac) made his winter home back in the years when Utah—or

15

Deseret as the Mormons called it—was still a nation to itself, far beyond reach of the Gentiles.

Another part of the American Desert now appears. We are leaving behind the monumental mesas, the labyrinthine canyons, the fantasy shapes and colors of the Colorado River country and entering what geographers call the Basin and Range Province, where the rivers flow not to the Pacific or Atlantic but into desert sands, evaporating in landlocked and brackish sumps like Pyramid Lake in Nevada and the Great Salt Lake in western Utah.

From above the southwest corner of Utah, looking ahead into Nevada, we can plainly note the transition. Instead of canyons, mesas, plateaus and the sculptured forms of sandstone we see long, forested mountain ranges trending north and south, each range isolated from the next by an intervening broad valley or "basin" of dun-colored desert—true wastelands of sparse, scrubby vegetation, wide beds of waterless drainages, huge alluvial fans spreading out from the base of each mountain into the valley below. The mountains stand half-buried in their own debris, the valleys marked by the winding subsurface rivers seeking an outlet, which most will never reach, to the sea.

The aspect below is one of unrelieved bleakness and barrenness—tawny sands, dull clays and gravels, gray rocky peaks and craggy breaks thinly covered with the olive drab of juniper and pinyon pine—but the scale of things is awesome, with even a city like Las Vegas, soon to come in view, only a minor variation on the general theme of emptiness, non-humanness, desolation. A grim scene to a man on foot or horseback, attempting with insufficient preparation and understanding to find his way to the next oasis. To the modern traveler, however, insulated as he is from all but the slightest chance of danger and discomfort, the vast shelterless expanse of these desert valleys can suggest a quality more interesting than threat of hardship: the grandeur of the terrible. The emotional catharsis, as Aristotle explained, of that which inspires terror without directly impinging upon our immediate well-being. The aesthetic of the desert. For some of those who have learned not only to live in but also to love the desert, it offers rewards greater than its visual appeal to the sense of beauty—the promise implicit in all that rugged wildness, that open, unfenced, untrammeled space—the sense of adventure, the reality of freedom, the hope of a refuge, if ever needed, from an ever expanding, excessively complex industrial culture which seems year by year to come always closer to internal collapse, terrorism, civil war. Or to what would be even worse, the absolute technological despotism of our contemporary nightmares.

Nightmares. Bad dreams. Of course it cannot happen here, not in America. Impossible. Banking north around the air space of Nellis Air Force Base—off limits to civilian aircraft—I gladly return the controls to T. K. Arnold. We circle in on the bright lights (already glowing through the evening smog), the foolish pleasures, and the strictly authorized craziness of this neon oasis known as Las Vegas. Not far away, northwest, is the Pentagon's proving grounds at Yucca Flats, where the preparations for the ultimate war have been carried on since 1945. What lies beyond that? Only a terrestrial paradise, as we all know: California, groaning under its burden of wealth, suffocating in its plentitude. The end of the open road.

Desert Images

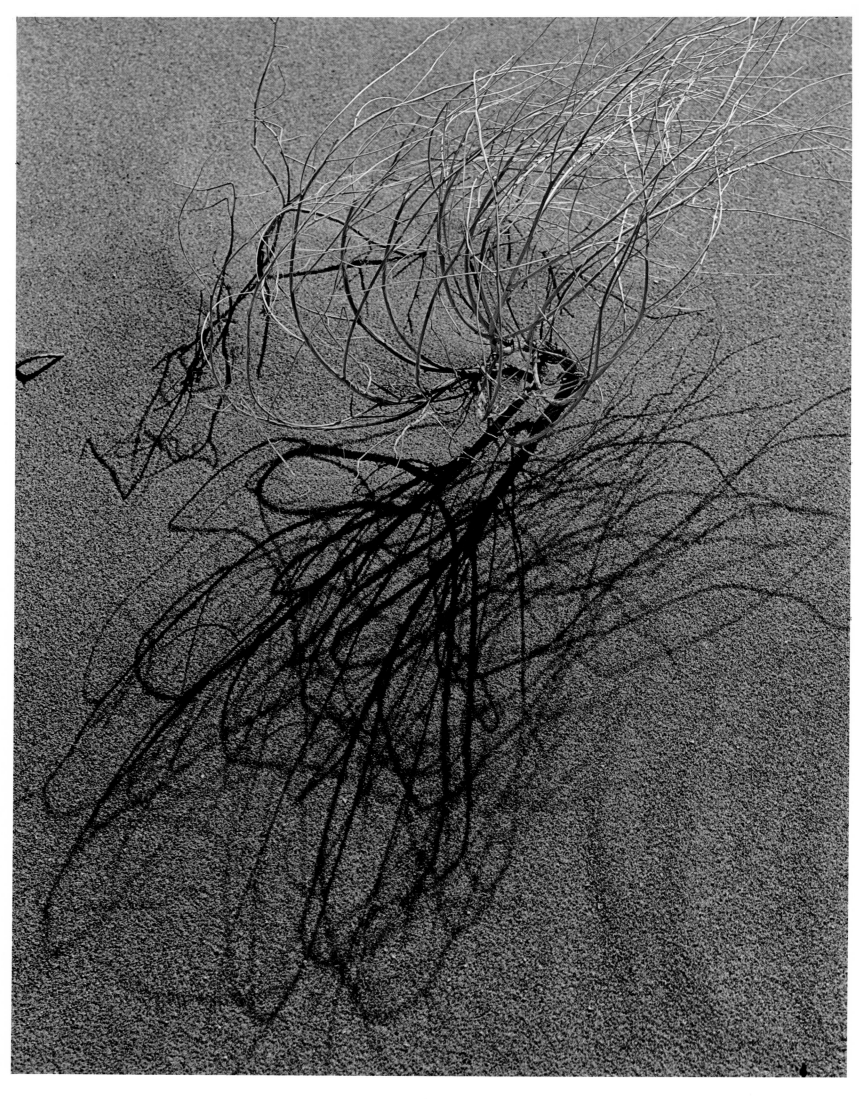

20

*Twisted, dry stalks, the
remains of a desert annual
that blossomed for a few
weeks, anchor a tiny patch of
sand in Nevada's Smokey
Valley dunes.*

Of all natural forms the sand dunes are the most elegant, so simple, severe, bare. Nature in the nude. Nothing can mar for long their physical integrity. Broken down by foot traffic, or machines, the sand is re-formed by the winds into fresh new dunes, formally perfect, advancing with the winds across the desert, where nothing but a mountain range can halt their progress.

Sand—unlike dust—is not airborne at great altitudes. Students of the matter have learned that even the strongest winds can seldom lift sand more than a foot or two above the ground. Where the ground is hard and fairly flat, however, the wind steady, the supply of sand sufficient, this lifting power is enough to form dunes.

A dune may begin with any obstacle on the surface—a stone, a shrub, a log, anything heavy enough to resist being moved by the wind. This obstacle forms a "wind shadow" on its leeward side, resulting in eddies in the current of the air, exactly as a rock in a stream causes an eddy in the water. Within the eddy the wind moves with less force and velocity than the airstreams on either side, creating what geologists call "the surface of discontinuity." Here the wind tends to drop part of its load of sand. The sand particles, which should be visualized as hopping or bouncing along the surface before the wind (not flying through the air), begin to accumulate, the pile grows higher, becoming itself a barrier to the wind, creating a greater eddy in the air currents and capturing still more sand. The formation of a dune is under way.

Viewed in cross section, sand dunes display a characteristic profile. On the windward side the angle of ascent is low and gradual—20 to 25 degrees from the horizontal. On the leeward side the slope is much steeper, usually about 34 degrees—the angle of repose of sand and most other loose materials. The steep side of the dune is called the slip face because of the slides that take place as sand is driven up the windward side and deposited on and just over the crest. When the deposit on the crest becomes greater than can be supported by the sand beneath, the extra sand slumps down the slip face. As the process is repeated through the years, the whole dune advances with the direction of the prevailing wind, until some obstacle like a mountain intervenes. At this point the dunes, prevented from advancing, pile higher. At Death Valley and in Great Sand Dunes

21

Sand Dunes

National Monument in Colorado the highest dunes reach five hundred feet. The only higher sand dunes are in Iran, where they attain a world's record of seven hundred feet.

Seen from the bird's point of view, most of these desert sand dunes have a crescent shape, like the new moon. The horns of the crescent point downwind with the slip face on the inside of the curve. This type of dune is called a *barchan*—an Arabic term. (A sea of sand, as in the Gran Desierto near the mouth of the Colorado River, is called an *erg*, another word borrowed from the Arabs, who have been dealing with these phenomena for a long time.) Dunes sometimes take other forms. There are transverse dunes, ridges of sand lying at a right angle to the course of the wind, and longitudinal dunes, which lie parallel to the wind. And there are parabolic dunes— barchans in reverse. Why dunes assume these different shapes poses a question not yet resolved by those who have pondered the problem.

How fast does a sand dune move? About twenty-five feet, sometimes up to fifty feet, in a year. Eventually the dunes achieve a point where they can advance no further, climb no higher. When this happens, they resume the equally ancient process of consolidating themselves into sandstone. Into rock. We are talking here of a leisurely natural process, of time periods longer than any human experience. Thousands of years. Millions of years. Sand and rock may observe a cosmic timetable, may follow some kind of pulse of their own, but if so this lies beyond human comprehension.

In our traditional conception of the desert we imagine it consisting entirely of billowing seas of sand, with here and there a palm tree, a gaunt saguaro cactus, the skull of a cow emerging from the sandy waves. Not so. Most of the Great American Desert is made up of bare rock, rugged cliffs, mesas, canyons, mountains, separated from one another by broad flat basins covered with sun-baked mud and alkali, supporting a sparse and measured growth of sagebrush or creosote or saltbush, depending on location and elevation. In the American Desert sand dunes are rather rare, relative to the size of the area of which they are a part. Death Valley; the San Luis Valley in Colorado; Monument Valley in Arizona and Utah; the White Sands of New Mexico; the sand dunes near Yuma, Arizona

22 and in the Mojave Desert of southern California; a few places

in Nevada—that sums it up. But like many things that are rare, a field of dunes makes up in beauty what it lacks in expanse.

A simple but always varied beauty. Shades of color that change from hour to hour—bright golden in morning and afternoon, a pallid tan beneath the noon sun, platinum by moonlight, blue-sheened under snow, metallic silver when rimed with hoarfrost, glowing like heated iron at sunrise and sunset, lavender by twilight. With forms and shapes, volumes and masses inconstant as wind but always lovely. Dunes like nude bodies. Dunes like standing waves. Dunes like arcs and sickles, scythe blades and waning moons. Virgin dunes untracked by machines, untouched by human feet. Dunes firm and solid after rain, ribbed with ripple marks from the wind. Dunes surrounding ephemeral pools of water that glitter golden as tiger's eye in the light of dawn. The clear-cut cornice of a dune, seen from below, carving out of the intense blue of the sky a brazen, brassy arc of monumental particulars. Yes—and the dunes that flow around and upon a dying mesquite tree in the Mojave, suffocating a stand of junipers and yellow pine in some lovely piece of back-country Utah. Sand and beauty. Sand and death.

All very pretty, the critic might agree, but what you are describing is a merely aesthetic response to natural appearances, an emotional luxury we can no longer afford in a world where basic human needs grow more desperate every year. Level those sands, the hard-nosed humanitarian will add; bring in water and plant the wastelands in sorghum, soybeans, alfalfa; make the desert blossom like a truck farm. We must provide more to the hungry than a pretty picture. There are answers to these objections, but they are not easy or simple. It is not enough to say that a man, or a child, does not live by bread alone. Beauty is a kind of food, a necessity for the soul—as all human cultures, without exception, have found—but it fills no bellies. You cannot offer a starving child a handful of sand.

But while time remains, we put these grim thoughts aside and go for a walk on the dunes. There may not be many years left. I leave the road and walk out on the dunes, following the delicate footprints of a fox. Past the arrowweed on the salt flats, past the little bosks of mesquite in the foothills of the dunes, up the windward side along the crest where the sand is so firm my feet leave only a faint impression. Following the fox. On the sand are other tracks even more dainty than those of the fox—the imprints of mice, beetles, lizards, birds.

I trail my fox into the lifeless heart of Death Valley, wondering where he might be bound. The morning sun rises higher above the purple Grapevine Mountains on the east, illuminates with a rosy glow the Panamint Mountains on the west. The tracks go high, then descend, then climb still higher on the next and greater dune. In general, with all its wandering, the fox seems to be bearing toward the highest dune of them all, four hundred feet above the valley floor. That fox should be hungry; a fox in the wild lives mostly on the keen edge of starvation. Yet his course is leading him farther and farther from any likely source of food. The fox's prey live below, among the clumps of vegetation between the dunes; the tracks of rodents and lizards become scarce, then nonexistent, as we climb higher.

Maybe this fox is crazy. Or rabid. Or old and looking for a place to die. Or a sightseer like me. Why the summit of the sands?

Yet that is where the trail finally leads me. To the high point of the highest dune. And there, as I can plainly read on the open page of the sand, the fox paused for a while, turning in one place, before plunging over the cornice and down, in great leaps, through the soft, unstable sand of the slip face, disappearing into the brush on the flats below.

What brought that fox up here? I don't know. A light wind is blowing now and all tracks, including my own, are beginning to soften, blur, fade out in a serried pattern of ripples in the sand. I lie belly down on the cornice of the dune, looking over the edge. Fine grains of sand, backlit by the sun, shining like particles of light, are swirling in the air. I can hear them tinkling and chiming as they fall on the sand below. Like crystals of quartz; like tiny fragments of broken glass. There is no other sound in this desert world.

I roll over on my back and gaze up at the cloudless, perfect, inhuman and unsheltering sky. The inevitable vulture soars there, a thousand feet above me. Black wings against the blue. I think I know that bird. He looks familiar. I think he's the one that's been following me, everywhere I go in the desert, for about thirty years. Looking after me. I follow the fox. The vulture follows me.

25

A winter sunrise colors the Mesquite Flat dunes in the lee of the Panamint Mountains of the Mojave Desert in California. On the horizon are the Grape-vine Mountains. The softly molded dunes tell of a mild winter without severe north winds.

26

Above. Rippling patterns in the Mesquite Flat dunes result from the constant interplay of the sand and wind. After a rare desert rain the sand can be quite firm.
Right. Sand patterns characteristic of the Mojave Desert are formed by prevailing winds in the Mesquite Flat dunes.
Overleaf. Only a major obstacle such as a mountain range can halt the march of these Mesquite Flat dunes at a rate of 25 or even 50 miles a year.

30

Above. A dune in Mesquite Flats topped by a clump of sparse vegetation forms a sort of wind break. Despite the appearance of desolation, various rodents, lizards, and birds may find a temporary home here.

Above. A clear view of both the windward and leeward sides of the Mesquite Flat dunes. The windward side is a gradual incline, but the leeward slope (the "slip-face") is steep because slides occur here as the dune becomes top-heavy.

Left. The lines of these dunes at the base of Tin Mountain in Death Valley National Monument seem fixed, but are constantly on the move before the wind.

Overleaf. Shaped by the moderate spring winds, the gradient is not sharply defined on the windward face of this dune in the Mesquite Flat area. The Grapevine Mountains loom beyond.

Below. Winter winds carved choppy ridges in the sand at Monument Valley, Arizona; later, gentler winds overlaid these with a smoother riffling pattern. Sandstone buttes offer a sharp contrast in the background.
Right. Branching ripples on a dune in Monument Valley Navajo Tribal Park probably result from random wind currents.

First Overleaf. Eerie sandstone skyscrapers, the Yebechei Rocks, including the magnificent, 1,000-foot-high Totem Pole on the right, rise above the desert floor in Monument Valley.
Second Overleaf. April storm winds from the west smother a landscape of low gypsum dunes. The gypsum particles have been blown in from the dried bed of Lake Lucero in White Sands National Monument, New Mexico. The San Andrea Mountains are on the skyline.

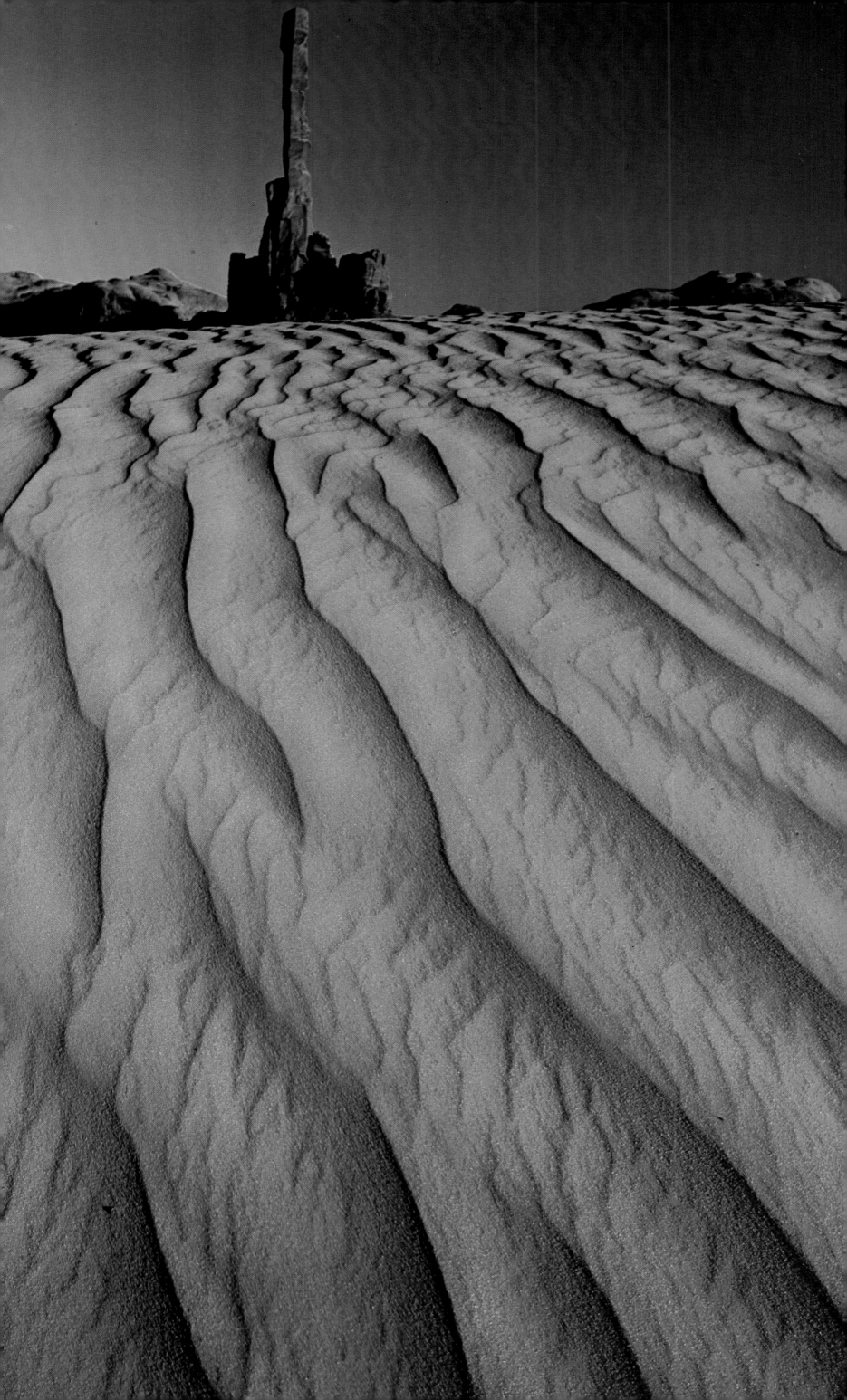

*Left. Yucca plants thrive on
the rolling fringe dunes at
White Sands National Monument. Although their hold
seems tenuous, these hardy
desert plants are well adapted
to extreme temperature shifts
and scarcity of water.
Above. Gypsum crystals are
ground into sand by the
elements, and the crystals,
shaped by the wind, form
rippling dunes in White Sands
National Monument.
Overleaf. These sand dunes in
White Sands National Monument are rarer in the American
desert than is commonly
believed; much of the desert
is bedrock.*

41

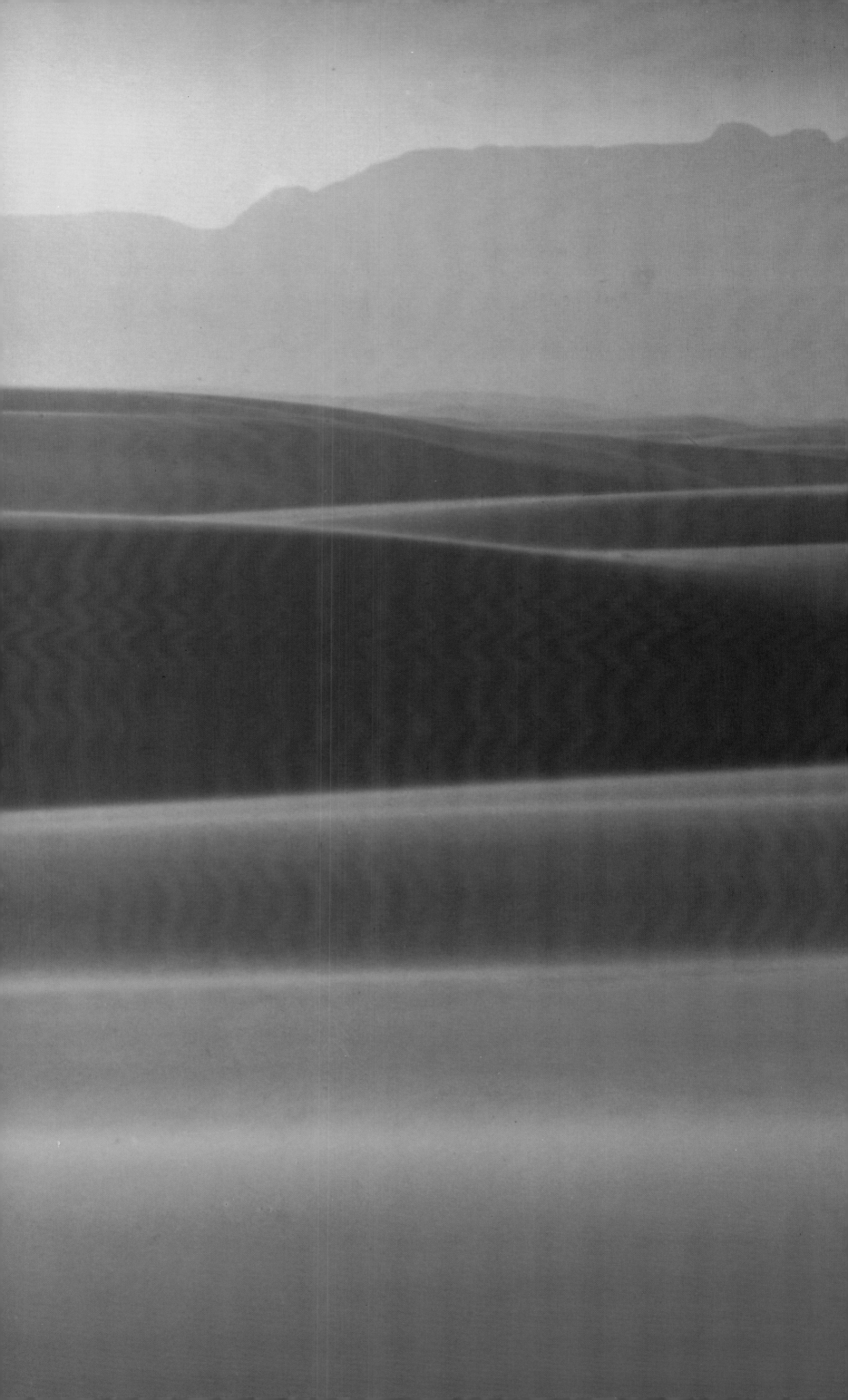

44

The Rio Grande River has channeled a deep gorge, the Santa Elena Canyon, through the heart of the limestone-layered rock. On the right bank is Big Bend National Park, Texas; on the left bank are cliffs bordering the Chihuahuan Desert in New Mexico.

"I love all things that flow," said James Joyce. "If there is magic on this earth it lies in water," Loren Eiseley said. And nowhere is water so beautiful as in the desert, for nowhere else is it so scarce. By definition. Water, like a human being or a tree or a bird or a song, gains value by rarity, singularity, isolation. In a humid climate, water is common. In the desert each drop is precious.

Way down in a corner of Arizona, near the Mexican border, is a tiny spring called Sweet Water. This spring is the only permanent, reliable, natural source of water between Quitobaquito on the east and the Tinajas Altas (high tanks) on the west—a distance of sixty miles by road. That road, surfaced in sand alternating with long stretches of blue-black lava rock, was called the Devil's Road— El Camino del Diablo. Accurate enough. Long since abandoned, bypassed by paved highways to the north and south, the Devil's Road can still be followed here and there, the route identifiable by dim tracks across the stone, by castoff wagon-wheel rims and antique Ford mufflers dissolving in rust, and by the mounds of stones and iron crosses that mark the burial sites of those who never made it. No one with any brains ever traveled that road in summer. In winter the low desert can be comfortable, even exhilarating, if you're properly equipped for survival; but in summer it is intolerable. The shimmer of heat waves, hanging like a scrim across the horizon, up from the basaltic rock toward the fiery furnace in the sky, is enough in itself to confuse the senses, puzzle the mind. The arid wind sucks moisture from every pore; the mountains float like ships on the waves of superheated air, drifting away from one another, then returning, merging, inverting themselves, assuming shapes out of fantasy. The madness of mirage.

Some of those passing on that road must have wondered, as they endured the heat and the thirst, what lay within the folds of a certain small mountain range to the south. A typical desert range: blue hills prickly with cactus, agave, spiny shrubs and stinging nettles, mostly bare of any vegetation at all, scaled and plated with loose rock, the high ridges notched with points like a dragon's backbone. What a few men knew was that there was water in there—the spring, Sweet Water. Not that the knowledge would have done the travelers much good. The spring is far from the road, difficult to reach; the effort required to get there might have taken more lives than the

45

Scarce Waters

little trickle of water could have saved. In the desert it is usually more important to ration bodily energy than water itself; sweat may be as costly as blood.

One morning in March I drove my government Jeep into the area, through the cactus forest, to the end of the dim track, then walked the last few miles. I had plenty of water, with me and within me; this was a pleasure jaunt. And part of my job as well; I was being paid to patrol these parts, investigate worked-out gold mines, check out game trails, inspect animal droppings, test the water of hidden tanks and secret springs.

There is no man-made trail, only a deer path, a bighorn sheep path, a lion run, leading to the spring. The stones are loose and tricky, the drop-offs vertical, the brush and cactus thick, resistant, hostile. One proceeds with care. A broken leg could be a serious mistake now, especially when alone. Accidents are forbidden. But the birds like it here: I was serenaded on my way by the sharp whistles of a thrasher — that signal so human-like that the first few times you hear it you always stop and look around, expecting to see a boy or another man. Or a woman, now that women have liberated themselves from certain genteel constraints. ("Whistling girls and crowing hens," my grandmother used to say, "both shall come to no good ends.")

Other birds are also present. I heard a cactus wren, its voice like the chatter of a rusty adding machine. And the sweet brief tunes of cardinal, pyrrhuloxia, phainopepla — the last a shy and rather furtive little bird, hard to get to know.

I reached a saddle in the mountains without finding the spring, though the convergence of tracks left by many small feet suggested that I was getting close. Plus the variety of scat on the trail: not only bighorn sheep and deer but also coyote, rabbit, kit fox, and the messy little clots of dung of the javelina, the wild pig or peccary of the Southwestern deserts. None of it, however, was fresh, except the sheep droppings. But that was encouragement enough.

Once on the other side of the saddle, and around a few more overhangs of rotten volcanic rock, and through a tunnel in the thorny mesquite and catclaw acacia, where I crawled on hands and knees to save the shirt from being torn off my back, I found the spring. It was easy to spot: a clump of leafless but conspicuously coppery

46 willows, a dwarf cottonwood barely beginning to leaf out with the

soft green of a new growing season. The little trees made only a patch of deciduous life in the midst of square miles of blue stone and olive-drab desert growth, but that single tiny patch was sufficient to indicate the presence of the desert's sweetest miracle: surface water. Or at the least, water very close to the surface. About fifty yards short of the spring and a little above it, downwind from the prevailing westerlies, I came upon a man-made sun shelter, or blind, of saguaro ribs. The structure looked immeasurably old but was held together with rusted wire, not natural fibers; it seems a safe guess it was made by Americans or Mexicans, not by Indians. Here the hunters would wait, for hours or days, perhaps, until game arrived. I squatted down in the meager shade of the thing, also prepared to wait, armed with binoculars, notebook, a canteen of water, a hunk of longhorn cheese, a box of raisins.

The sun went down. I put on my coat as the temperature dropped ten, fifteen, twenty degrees within twenty minutes. Binoculars ready, I watched the water hole—the only water hole within twenty miles. The bird songs faded away. Two or three crickets began to rub their forewings together down by the spring. The lavender dusk, in a precipitation of colors too subtle to name, spread across the desert hills, through the sky, across Sonora to the south, across the fifty miles of landscape within my range of sight. The sickle moon grew brighter.

Most desert animals do not require water daily. The deer, the bighorn sheep, the javelina, are believed (no one knows for certain) able to go two or three days at a time without a drink, getting by, that is, on what they've stored in their tissues. Early March, also, is not the best of times for finding wildlife at a water hole; cool days, natural tanks full of winter rains, fresh plant growth make needs less pressing. Midsummer—July, August, September—that's the time. It was quite possible, therefore, that I would see nothing.

I waited. The air grew chillier, the moon slipped lower, the night came on. One more hour, I resolved, and then I give up; then it's back up the trail by moonlight and down the other side, back to the Jeep, a beer, something hot to eat, before laying out my bedroll on the desert floor.

I heard the clash of stone far down in the brush-filled ravine below the spring. I raised the field glasses and studied the area but could

47

see nothing in motion. I waited, changing position again to ease my aching limbs. Again I heard the slight, faint, far-off click of something hard on stone. An animal was approaching and as I watched, concentrating on the mesquite and acacia thickets, I saw first one then a second sleek, gracile, dun-colored form appear, climbing on delicate hoofs up the path toward the spring. Followed by a third, a fourth, a fifth, all in single file. And then two more. And still more, at least a dozen in all, quiet as shadows, pale and obscure as the twilight, bodies barely distinguishable from their mottled background of stone and brush.

For a moment I thought they were small deer. But all young bucks! With black spikes. And then I recognized them as desert pronghorn, a species almost extinct in the United States, though once quite numerous in southern Arizona. These had probably come up from Mexico, sliding under the fence like illegal immigrants. I was glad to see them. They gathered about the spring, jostling one another until the basic order of precedence was re-established, then drank, two or three at a time while the others waited and watched. I could hear the gurgling of water passing rapidly down those parched throats, the sighs and grunts of satisfaction. There is something in the feeding and drinking of large animals that gives, to the human onlooker, a sensation of deep pleasure. Mammalian empathy, perhaps. Finally the pronghorns had enough. A long time, as it seemed to me, for of course I had to wait until the last had drunk before I could stir; I didn't want to scare away from a much needed watering even the lowest pronghorn in the pecking order. Not until all turned and started back the way they'd come did I stand up. At once, with a clatter of stones and armored feet, they took off. A dozen white rump patches flashed in the moonlight. Vanishing two seconds later into the gloom below—soon gone beyond earshot as well as sight.

I inspected the spring. A ring of dampness showed that the pronghorns had lowered the water level eight inches. I felt the muddy residue, then cupped my hands under the trickle that flowed from the algae-covered rock, and drank. Good, cool, soft water. . . .

Satisfied I followed the path back to the saddle of the mountain, through the moonlit tangle of cactus and brush, over the rocks, back to my headquarters for the night.

48

49

Above. Drought has lowered the water level of Desert Creek at Tortilla Flat in the Superstition Wilderness of Arizona, exposing the creek bed.

First Overleaf. One of seven cascades in Bear Creek, Catalina Mountains, Arizona. When snow melts on the southern exposure, torrents of water cause flash floods in the desert washes below. Second Overleaf. These sandstone monoliths in Monument Valley, Arizona, have been likened to a king on his throne, a stagecoach, a bear, and a rabbit. Navajo sheep drink from a rainpool in the foreground.

*Left. At Lower Deer Creek
Falls along the Colorado River,
in Arizona, a spring-fed creek
has carved a winding gorge
through sandstone cliffs.
Above. Red Rock Crossing in
Oak Creek Canyon, Arizona,
glows in the light of a
November sunrise, outlining
dramatic buttes and mesas
characteristic of this terrain.*

*Below. The Amargosa River,
fed by the Tecopa Hot Springs,
swollen by abnormally heavy
rains, enters the ordinarily dry
basin of Death Valley,
California.*

*Right. Badwater Pool at
sunrise mirrors the scenery of
Telescope Peak in Death
Valley, where the terrain
rises—at this point—from
282 feet below sea level to
11,045 feet above.*

56

*First Overleaf. Below Dante's
View in Death Valley, three or
four Amargosa River channels
merge around Badwater Pool
just south of the lowest
elevation in the United States.
Second Overleaf. Rains from a
Baja California hurricane
flood Silver Dry Lake, one of
a chain of Mojave Desert lakes
that once emptied into the
Amargosa River.*

*Third Overleaf. Elaborate tiers
of stalactites line the entrance
to the King's Palace, part of
the world's largest caverns, at
Carlsbad Caverns National
Park, New Mexico.*

64

*A brittlebush plant
grows among granite boulders
on an alluvial wash in Anza-
Borrego State Park, California.*

Rock? Rocks? For God's sake what more is there to say about rocks? They're hard. They're old. They're dangerous. Here in the desert they shelter scorpions, which lurk beneath them during the day and scuttle over them at night—usually when you're trying to clear a smooth place to lay your sleeping bag. Rocks work loose in your hand when you're climbing, crack and slide under your boots, come ricocheting at forty miles an hour off the ledge above your skull. Into your teeth. Let's talk about something else.

Of course they are great fun to roll. The best rock rolling I've known was at Lava Cliffs in the Grand Canyon. Off Cape Solitude into Marble Gorge. Down from the rim into Ubehebe Crater, Death Valley. Off the knife-edge ridge leading to the summit of Sierra Blanca in Colorado. Down from the outlyers of the Sierra Carmen above Big Bend, Texas. Or best of all the tremendous slab that a friend and I dislodged, with the aid of a log for leverage, from the rim of Dead Horse Point, Utah—a free fall of eight hundred feet; that two-ton monolith *exploded* into dust; the reverberations, seven years later, are even yet echoing off the cliffs from Upheaval Dome to Anticline Overlook, faint but detectable with scientific instruments. Nothing in our universe is wholly lost.

Horseplay. Rock can be a little more serious. Only a year ago a façade of sandstone weighing approximately fifty tons spalled off the canyon wall above a cove in Lake Powell, Utah. Nothing new in that; since the formation of this reservoir by Glen Canyon Dam the canyon walls have been slumping into the water regularly and frequently. What made this incident special was that a thirty-foot cabin cruiser happened to be underneath at the time; neither boat nor bodies were ever recovered.

One day a friend and I were hiking around Navajo Mountain, near the Utah-Arizona border. Following the trail down a winding 1,000-foot slit in the plateau called Cliff Canyon we paused to rest in the shade of a solitary juniper. Meditating there, subsiding into sleep, we were startled wide awake by a sound like the end of the world: an avalanche of rock crashing into the canyon around the next bend, hardly a hundred feet from where we lay. The rockfall, as we found a minute later, had completely buried a section of the trail, precisely the section we'd have been walking on had we not stopped to rest. To what did we attribute our miraculous salvation? Pure luck.

Rough Rock

So far I've been talking about loose rock, missiles, falling objects impelled by mischief or erosion. But the striking thing about the desert country is of course the great peaks and pinnacles, arches and windows and bridges, massifs and mountains, capitol domes and volcanic necks, the infinite variety of queer misshapen forms that solid rock can take when exposed to the weathering work of the elements and given a liberal allowance of time. Vast surfaces of the desert consist of almost nothing but bare rock, continuous monolithic rock, miles and leagues of solid rock, with here and there in the crevices a pocket of sand supporting a pinyon pine, a clump of scrub oak stabilizing a dune of coral-pink sand.

The rock forms loom up gigantically against the sky. So huge, steadfast, enduring, it seems natural to attribute to them such qualities as nobility . . . serenity . . . and so on. Pathetic fallacies, no doubt. Yet the temptation to imagine something of that sort is irresistible. Contemplating one of the great sandstone towers of Monument Valley, one easily fantasizes that the tower is also engaged in contemplation. But not of human affairs. The life span of the rock must be measured in hundreds of thousands of years. What the great rocks contemplate, therefore, as Robinson Jeffers said of the Pacific, "is not our wars."

Absurd, of course. Stone is mere brute matter, insentient, utterly incapable of feeling, knowing, seeing. So it seems to us, in our short human lives. One merely suggests a certain crazy hypothesis: that things which stand in one place for an entire geologic age may — somehow — exert some kind of dim force upon their surroundings. That maybe they are more than simply the passive objects of weathering and erosion.

Some of the towers resemble Egyptian gods — manlike forms five hundred feet tall, with the heads and beaks of predatory birds. In volcanic regions, as in the Superstition Mountains of Arizona, stand the cores or plugs of vanished volcanoes; these may take the form of craggy spires — Weaver's Needle brooding over the surrounding landscape of desert wilderness — or Shiprock on the Navajo reservation in northwestern New Mexico, visible (before the coal-burning powerplants at Four Corners) from fifty or sixty miles away. One thousand four hundred feet high, Shiprock presented a special challenge to serious rock climbers; it was considered one of the ten most difficult climbs in the United States. Finally it began to attract so many climbers that the Navajo Indians, for whom the rock is a sacred place, banned all climbing. Only the golden eagles perch there now, and the red-tailed hawks, and perhaps a few less tangible and mortal things.

Of the many lovely things in the desert, one of the loveliest is a channel carved by running water in solid bedrock. In hundreds of little canyons across the Southwest you'll find these curious drainages where water, steady or intermittent, has sculptured the stone into shapes like the work of Henry Moore. Grooves, chutes, slides, tunnels, basins, plunge pools, potholes, all as smooth as marble and equally slippery, all part of the same undivided, monolithic rock. There is a canyon in Utah called Death Hollow because of the cattle that have died in there, entering to drink the water in the deep pools, then unable to climb out. Waterpocket Fold, also in Utah, is a long monocline containing many such sculptured canyons of unbroken stone.

The rock is not entirely lifeless. Junipers, pinyon pines, yucca, cactus, grow from tiny fissures in the rock. Here and there are depressions where enough blown sand has collected to support a garden of Indian rice grass, cliff rose, prickly pear and juniper. But each little garden may be separated from the next by a hundred yards of bare rock without any plant life at all.

Miles of stone beneath the sun. There are places in Utah, Arizona, Nevada, where a man could walk for twenty-five miles without leaving a single discernible footprint on the earth. Only a hound could track you across that wilderness fantasy in stone. Stone walls with natural windows; alcoves and amphitheaters big enough for the New York Philharmonic and an audience of ten thousand; great curving arches and bridges of rose-colored sandstone enclosing a view of the sky, the sun, the stars, the moon, whatever lies beyond; fields of granite boulders rising toward the buttresses of the Sierra Nevada; broad sun-baked near-level wastelands of small stones fitted to one another like the tiles on a bathhouse floor—"desert pavement," it's called—with the surface tarnished by air and chemistry to the hue of rusted iron; the stone throats of wine-stem canyons polished by a million years of flashflooding to a finish slick as glass, inlaid with a mosaic of vari-colored jewels resembling garnets, jasper, amethysts, rubies,

opals, ivory, crystal. . . . All quite worthless, of course. Useless
on the living room mantel; out of place on the shelves of your
picture window, among the potted plants, dead flies, old wine stains.
Good only for looking at, for rubbing your hand upon, for
marveling over.

Slickrock. Out back of beyond, where nothing grows and the wind
always blows. One pioneer woman, after surviving the historic
1879-80 Hole-in-the-Rock trek from Escalante to Bluff, in southern
Utah, described what she had seen in these words: "Nothing but
hills and holes and humps and hollows."

Hills like melted elephants. Hills like crumbling castles. Buttes like
skyscraper pipe organs. Cathedrals of stone, carved by wind and
rain and frost and ice into an intricate tracery of lace and filigree,
with gargoyles out of a gothic nightmare squatting on surreal
pedestals of petrified mud. Moonlight scenes to horrify the innocent.
Visions of eternity frozen in stone, hallucinations fixed in rock
specters, enough to jolt the most hardened opium eater into permanent
insanity—or back to earth. "Rock forms that we do not understand,"
wrote Major John Wesley Powell, an early explorer of the Southwestern deserts. But persisting, he did come to understand them,
as have a thousand students in the century since Powell's early
journey. For all its incredible, seemingly incomprehensible
complexity and variety of shape, color, and substance, the
character of rock follows logical patterns. Erosion, weathering,
gravity, granular structure, bonding and bedding: the axioms
that provide the foundations of geomorphology are rather
few and simple. All known observations support the basic principle:
uniformity of change under certain given conditions must always take
place, given a sufficient length of time. Where little vegetation can
grow the underlying structure is nakedly revealed. Remove the flesh
of plant life ("All flesh is grass") and the bones of the earth lie plain
and exposed.

It is not necessary to understand the doctrines of science in order to
enjoy the presence of rocks. Of rock. The most blandly and stubbornly
ignorant, peering for the first time over the rim of the Grand Canyon,
are bound to say, or at least to feel: "Something happened here."
Rock gives reality to the otherwise abstract notion of transhuman
68 time. Touch the canyon wall and you touch the bedrock of earthly being.

69

Above. Sandstone concretions
in Anza-Borrego Park's
"Pumpkin Patch" range across
the desert floor.

Overleaf. The light from a
waning storm outlines the
eroding granite of the Alabama
Hills in California's Sierra
Nevadas.

Right. The spiny ridges of Emigrant Canyon in Death Valley are gradually being leveled by erosion.
First Overleaf. The mud hills of Death Valley's Twenty Mule Canyon, formed in the Cenozoic era, are eroded by weather and scorched by the sun.
Second Overleaf. At the Race Track, near the faulted Paleozoic limestone out-croppings of the Cottonwood Mountains in Death Valley, isolated rocks form a permanent ridge.

Above. At the northern end of Death Valley National Monu-ment, in California, the rigid contours of Ubehebe Crater are slowly being worn down by wind, sand, and weathering.

Left. The twisted profiles of metamorphic rock formations line Grotto Canyon in Death Valley.
Right. Heavy rains washed rocky debris down to the foot of the Ubehebe Crater in Death Valley, forming a playa as the rainwater evaporates.
Below. A rock pattern chiseled by the elements deep in the bedrock of Marble Canyon in Death Valley.
Overleaf. The sandstone formations in the foreground offer a somber contrast to the fresh layer of January snow which covers the Virgin Mountains beyond, in Valley of Fire State Park, Nevada.

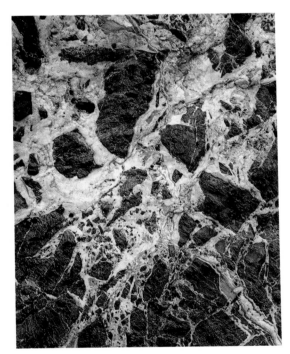

82

*Above. Sandstone "windows"
such as this one in Valley of
Fire are formed chiefly by
weathering.*

*Right. The same sandstone
"window," as the morning light
reveals the bedrock of the
desert floor and the bizarre
rock formations around it.
First Overleaf. Dried winter
hop sage is scattered over the
basins and ranges of the
Lunar Crater region in central
Nevada.
Second Overleaf. Near Dead
Horse Point, Utah, the Colorado
River meanders through
formations of Wingate sandstone above, creating a massive
canyon in the heart of the
plateau.*

First Overleaf. Sage- and juniper-studded flatlands stretch back to a sandstone tableau and the magnificent Yebechei Rocks, in Monument Valley, Arizona.
Second Overleaf. Left Mitten, a huge monolith in Monument Valley, stands in the soft light of an April moon.
Third Overleaf. Seen from the base of Bell Rock, a summer storm sweeps across the sandstone rim of Oak Creek Canyon, Arizona.
Fourth Overleaf. Volcanic remnants in the form of plugs, necks, and dikes line the border of the Navajo Trail in Arizona.
Fifth Overleaf. A pedestal log of petrified wood lies in the varicolored shale of the Petrified Forest in Arizona.

Above. A detailed view of the so-called Wonderstone found near Kanab, Utah.
Right. Traces of erosion are evident in the patterns on this sandstone formation on East Rim Trail, Zion National Park, Utah.

100

*Left. The same petrified log
here appears balanced on the
edge of a rocky promontory.
Right Above. Volcanic rock
pinnacles range across the
Heart of Rocks section of
Chiricahua National Monument,
Arizona.
Right Below. Lichen patterns
decorate the Navajo sandstone
of Comb Reef, Arizona.
First Overleaf. The northern
rim of the Grand Canyon as seen
from Desert Tower on the
south rim.
Second Overleaf. Another view
of these subtly shaded limestone ridges pitched against
a summer evening in Grand
Canyon National Park,
Arizona.*

*Left. The fibrous yucca, seen
here in Malpais lava beds in
Tularosa Valley, New Mexico,
is one of the few plants hardy
enough to survive on volcanic
rocks.
Below. The area south of
Shiprock in northwestern New
Mexico is studded with these
craggy volcanic dikes.*

107

*First Overleaf. Sand, wind
and water have carved out a
City of Rocks in New
Mexico's Chihuahuan Desert.
Second Overleaf. The City of
Rocks glistens in the sunrise
as the setting moon wanes.*

*A desert primrose in
solitary splendor at Anza-
Borrego State Park, California.*

Life is gaunt and spare in the desert; that's what old time desert rats like best about it. They feel they cannot breathe properly without at least a cubic mile of unshared space about them. Let another man or woman appear on their horizon and they begin to feel the urge to decamp, move on, climb yonder ridge, investigate that purple range of barren hills beyond the gleaming salt flats, find out at least what's going on up in there, among those shadowy valleys, those ragged battlements of broken-down rock. Where, as they should know damn well, they'll find nothing but the same scatter of dried-out brittlebush, the same fireplugs of barrel cactus with spines like fishhooks, the same herd of feral burros gaping at them from the ridgeline, the same dun-colored rattler coiled beneath a limestone shelf, waiting its chance to strike. Death in its glance.

Desert plant life is much the same: private. Even the commonest shrub, like the creosote bush, keeps its distance from the next. Each sets alone inside an ample circle of open ground. Botanists say that the roots of the plant secrete a poison, a growth inhibitor, that prevents new, seedling creosote from getting a start within that charmed circle of solitariness.

So it is with the flowers of the desert, though not without some exceptions. In certain years, not frequent, when the winter drizzles have fallen at the right times in the correct amounts, and when the weather achieves exactly the proper balance in March and April between heat and cold, sunlight and cloud-cover, you may be lucky enough to see whole desert valleys and hills covered, "carpeted" as they say, with a solid blaze of flowering Mexican poppy, or globe mallow, or mimulus or coreopsis. These are splendid and rare occasions, attracting flower freaks, photographers, and desert flora fanciers from half the cities of the nation, odd people who think nothing of grabbing a jet plane and flying two thousand miles to see the flare-up of sudden orange when the *Calochortus kennedyi* takes over some Mojave valley down in California's wastelands. That or the Mexican poppies. Or the brittlebush itself, an otherwise humble and obscure knee-high shrub, which can perform wonders: nothing could be more striking than to see one of the grim black cinder cones in the Pinacate lava fields take on suddenly—almost overnight—a rash of yellow, when twenty thousand brittlebushes break out in simultaneous golden bloom. Ridiculous. And sublime.

Wild Flowers

But these are, as said, the exceptions. Generally the flowers of the desert reveal themselves in solitary splendor. A primrose lurking on a sand dune. A single paloverde flaring by an arid watercourse. One woolly clump of *Baileya multiradiata* gracing the edge of the asphalt, shivering in the breeze from 40-ton freight trucks. The great *Agave palmeri* or century plant blooms only once in its entire existence ("the garland briefer than a girl's"), but in that supreme assertion of love and continuity it more than justifies the sacrifice required. For a decade or so the century plant grows, emerging slowly from the rock; the heavy spine-tipped blades that function as leaves wax fat, with an interlocking bulge in the center resembling an artichoke. Here the food and energy is stored. One spring a signal is given, we don't know what or why. The bulge unfolds, like a slow-motion explosion, and a shaft rises from the center, growing rapidly, reaching a height of ten or twelve feet within a week. This is the flower stalk, efflorescing as it rises with a series of alternate flower-bearing stems from midpoint to the top. The yellowish, heavy blooms wait there, upright on the towering stalk, for a week, two weeks, are pollinated by bats and insects, then begin to fade. As they fade the plant dies slowly, by degrees, from stem to root, though the strong, rigid shaft, supported by the base, may stand erect for a year after death. The death does not matter; the seeds have been sown.

The desert offers a second outburst of flowering in September and October, after the customary summer rains. This is the time of the globe mallow, the sore-eye poppy as it's also known, and chamiza (or rabbitbrush), a stinking shrub with a showy display of yellow bloom, and the sunflowers—acres and acres of waist-high mule-ear (so named for the shape of the leaves) *Helianthus annuus*, visible from miles away.

Down in dank and shady places grows a shady customer—angel's trumpet, the sacred *Datura inoxia*. A large gross ivory-colored thing, set amid dark and shiny green leaves, the whole plant, flowers, stem, leaves, roots, is rich in scopolamine, a potent alkaloid much prized by witch doctors. The correct dosage is said to be spiritually rewarding but the problem is that a microgram too much may lead to convulsions, paralysis, and death—also rewarding, perhaps, but

usually considered premature.

I try to think of a favorite among my arid-country flowers. But I love them all. How could we be true to one without being false to all the others? Just the same I think I'll praise a few more individuals here, single them out from among the crowd.

The cliff rose, for example. A flowering shrub, *Cowania mexicana*, a true member of the rose family, the cliff rose can be found in many parts of the mesa country and high desert from Colorado to California. The shrub may grow from four to twelve feet high. Twisted and gnarled like a juniper, it is relatively inconspicuous most of the year. But in April and May it blooms, putting out a thick, showy cluster of pale yellow or cream-colored flowers with the fragrance of orange blossoms. On a breezy day in spring you can smell the faint, delicate but heart-intoxicating sweetness for miles. The cliff rose is a bold plant, flourishing in the most improbable places, clinging to the cliff's edge, overhanging the rim of a plateau, gracing the pockets of sand far out among the slickrock domes. Deer, bighorn sheep, domestic sheep and cattle all browse on the leaves of this plant in the winter, when little else is available.

Or how about the wild morning glory, *Evolvulus arizonicus*? Another beauty. A hardy annual that blooms from April to October. The flowers are small, scarcely half an inch in diameter, but of so clear and striking an azure blue, especially in contrast to the tiny leaves and scraggly stems of the plant itself, that they assert themselves —against the sun-bleached background of sand and rock—with eye-catching vigor.

Several varieties of lupine grow in the desert. In Arizona the violet-purple *L. sparsiflorus*, in West Texas the blue-purple *L. havardii*, in southwest California the royal-purple *L. odoratus*. Bushy members of the pea family, the lupines generally grow from two to three feet tall in clusters along roadways, trails, and the edges of valley bottoms, wherever the runoff from rains tends to be a little heavier. Sometimes they grow in pure stands, turning the burnt umber and dun brown of the desert into a wind-shimmering lake of blue-pink-purple radiance. The lupine is not good for anything; hungry livestock eat them, get sick and die. (Alkaloids.) All they have to offer us is their own rare beauty.

One more. A secret flower, a hidden special, little known, seldom publicized: the desert prince's plume, *Stanleya pinnata*, a man-high plant that blooms from May to July in some of the hottest, dreariest, most God-forsaken and otherwise life-forsaken places in the South-west. In dried-out mud flats along arid watercourses; on the shale and gravel talus slopes under a Moencopi-formation rock bluff; around the alkaline edges of some desperate mudhole way out in the clay hills, the badlands, the Painted Desert. The flowers stand up in golden spikes, racemes of bright yellow blazing against the red cliffs and blue sky.

In those secret canyon glens where the hanging gardens grow, nourished on water percolating through the sandstone, you'll find yellow columbine. Certainly as beautiful a flower as anything on earth, though not so large and spectacular as the blue columbine of the mountains. Many others live here too, delicate as angel's breath, and tough. They've got to be tough, surviving in those precarious perches on a perpendicular slickrock wall.

And then you walk out in the badlands and see a single Indian paint-brush lifting its cup of salmon-colored, petal-like bracts toward the sky. The paintbrush too is beautiful, with the special and extra-ordinary beauty of wild and lonely things. Every desert flower shares that quality. Anything that lives where it would seem that nothing could live, enduring extremes of heat and cold, sunlight and storm, parching aridity and sudden cloudbursts, among burnt rock and shifting sands, any such creature—beast, bird or flower—testifies to the grandeur and heroism inherent in all forms of life. Including the human. Even in us.

117

*Above. Rabbit brush, wild rye,
and other desert plants cover
the great basin and range
area of Nevada's Spring Valley.*

Left. Yellowcups—or desert evening primroses—blossom at springtime below Corkscrew Park in Death Valley.
Top Right. A delicate desert lily survives under the desert sun in Anza-Borrego State Park.
Bottom Right. A desert holly pokes through a tiny fissure of slate in Marble Canyon in Death Valley's Cottonwood Range.

118

119

*Above. Bigelow mimulus puts
on a lavish display of color in
Borrego Palm Canyon in
Anza-Borrego State Park.
Right. Even at nightfall,
California poppies and thistle
sages brighten the floor of
Antelope Valley in the Mojave
Desert.*

Left. In spring, the Tehachapi foothills of the Mojave Desert blaze with Bigelow coreopsis. Right. A few desert stars are rooted in an alluvial wash at the base of the Grapevine Mountains in Death Valley. Overleaf. An alluvial wash at the base of California's Coyote Mountains yields a brilliant spread of dune primrose, marigolds, and a few sand verbena.

Above. A detail of the stubby strawberry hedgehog cactus in the Sonoran-Mojave Desert reveals the complexity of the inner plant.
Right. This coarse sandstone façade in Zion National Park, Utah, provides nourishment for a brave show of Indian paintbrush.

Left. In Arizona's Organ Pipe Cactus National Monument, golden California poppies mingle with desert primroses, both vying for nutrients and and moisture.
Right Above. Lush California poppies contrast with the spare branches of ocotillo in the foothills of the Ajo Mountains in Organ Pipe Cactus National Monument.
Right Below. A carpet of California poppies, cholla and brittlebush, and saguaro cactus stretches to the base of the Ajo Mountains.
Overleaf. The serrated volcanic ridges of the Ajo Range overshadow an expanse of gold California poppies.

129

132

Beavertail prickly pear, so named for the shape of the succulent pads, glows with spring color in Valley of Fire State Park, Nevada.

I saddled this big sorrel gelding we called Hook, seventeen hands tall, led him around inside the corral for a while, then slipped on quickly before he had time to think it over. He had a small brain with few thoughts, all of them evil. He was four years old. I hate to think what the beast would've been like if old Cliff Woods (tamer of horses) hadn't cut off his *cojones* when Hook was two weeks old. Once, I mounted that horse bareback without going through the preliminary circling ritual, and he tried to decapitate me by plunging beneath a sycamore limb. I saved my head by diving—for the first and last time—into a jojoba bush.

We went down over the bluff on a little rocky path, splashed across Aravaipa Creek, and rode up the wagon track under the sycamores. Splendid, monumental trees, dappled like pintos, with fat smooth limbs you could build a treehouse in. I'd sometimes climb one of those trees and sit up in there, deep in the green-gold shade, hiding from visitors I didn't want to see, or just to brood, or think, or write.

My horse behaved himself as we clopped along through passing spangles of sunlight and shadow. He was mean but not really dangerous so long as you stayed alert and kept a firm grip on the reins. Hook was built for speed, not comfort, and for mountain climbing, not relaxing. We had a three-thousand foot-climb ahead of us and a fifteen-mile round trip ride, good enough for one afternoon. I meant to be back by dark, have supper at home.

The trail left the creek bottom and climbed the first bench toward the mesa. Glancing below as we climbed, I looked right down on the tops of the giant saguaro cactus that grew on the rocky slope. On the crown of each trunk and each upraised arm was a cluster of creamy-white flowers. This was early June again; the saguaros were in bloom.

Up the long sloping bajada of rock, gravel and eroded alluvium toward the cliffs, we followed the old road, passing through a rock garden. Mesquite grew here, and paloverde, creosote, jojoba, and a dozen varieties of cactus: clock-face prickly pear; Engelmann's prickly pear; spiny clusters of hedgehog, shin-high to a man; fishhook cactus; pincushion cactus; barrel cactus; rainbow cactus; purplish buckhorn or Christmas cactus with little red berries; chain fruit cholla with its dangling joints; and the pale-gold, shining, cuddly-

Cactus Land

looking teddy bear cholla, meanest of the whole crew. Sometimes called jumping cholla, from the ease with which the prickly joints are detached by the slightest contact. They do seem to jump at you. Gotcha! Once impaled, you need a stick to dislodge the clinging joint. And pliers to remove the barbed needles, one by one. You'd be not much worse off playing with a porcupine.

Towering far above all other cactus, above the mesquite and paloverde trees as well, were the saguaros. The giant cactus. The tallest cactus in the world, some growing as high as fifty feet. The arch-symbol of the American desert, although actually typical of only one part of it—the Lower Sonoran life zone of southern Arizona and northwestern Mexico.

Great succulent plants, the saguaros are capable of storing tons of water after a heavy rain. This storage capacity enables them to survive the prolonged droughts that follow the brief rainy season of the desert. A widespread root system sucks up the moisture from the ground immediately after rain. The columnar trunk, with its fluted or pleated walls, expands to allow water-absorption by the sponge-like stem tissue, then slowly contracts during the dry spells that follow. Even in the driest years it produces fruit, scarlet cucumber-like objects much loved by birds and rodents, and formerly harvested, every year, by desert Indian tribes like the Papagos. Using long poles—saguaro ribs—the Papagos would break the fruit from the tops of the trunks and arms, gather and dry it, sometimes make a wine from the fermented pulp.

Woodpeckers pursuing insects drill holes in the saguaro; the same holes, sealed on the inside by the saguaro's healing powers, may later be used as nests by birds and by the miniature elf owl.

A saguaro lives about two hundred years. Its dying is a lengthy process, the fleshy hulk gradually disassembling itself, shredding off like leprous skin, gouts and gobs of rotten pulp hanging from body and arms. Eventually only the ribbed skeleton remains, turning slowly a pale tan under the sun. One day in a storm, a year, two years after its clinical death, the skeleton crashes to the ground.

My horse pranced up the mountain road. Strong and crazy, he'd run the whole way up if I let him, burst his huge eager heart through sheer exuberance, anger, stupidity. I kept him reined in to a fast walk on the upgrade, a steady trot across the level stretches.

Three white-tailed deer leaped from the trail and bounded away;
a herd of javelina, frantic, comic caricatures of piggery, went scrambling off at my approach, snorting into the brush. Which reminded me of my business here; I was game warden for a privately owned wildlife preserve. The daily patrol was part of the job; the poachers I was not seriously on the lookout for were some of my neighbors, both friends and enemies. A nice job, generally, but with difficult moments. Having loaded guns waved in your face, for example, by a pack of drunken pig hunters.

High up the side of the mesa, two thousand feet above the creek, we passed my favorite barrel cactus, a double-barreled freak, a mutant, a splurge of cell tissue running amuck. But the plant seemed healthy enough, growing tall as a man, and richly green.

Among outdoorsmen, porcupines have long been regarded as an easily taken emergency food supply. (Although they're never around when you need them.) And for that reason protected; to kill a porcupine for sport is taboo. The outdoorsmen of the Southwest—desert rats—cherish the barrel cactus for analogous reasons. Not as food but as a source of life saving moisture in an extreme situation. Water when none other is available.

As the name implies, the barrel cactus is a stout and heavy vegetable. Certain species may grow ten feet tall, though most that you'll encounter in the American Southwest do not exceed six feet. The proportions are not quite barrel-like but it is a thick, massive, single-branched, roughly cylindrical plant, armored with a dense growth of rigid red and yellow fishhook-like spines. (Botanists tell us that the spines function not only to protect the cactus from hungry animals but also to partly shade the plant while allowing free passage of air.) The first problem then is getting at the plant; leather gloves and a big machete would be helpful. But if you're desperate you'll manage with a rock, a club, a piece of iron. Knock off the top of the barrel cactus; inside you will find—not any liquid, of course—but the pale green, pulpy flesh of the plant. If it has recently absorbed water from a rain the flesh will contain, maybe, a helpful amount of moisture. Crush the pulp, squeeze out the water. Or chew it like a chunk of watermelon, sucking out the juice. Do not eat the pulp; old-timers say it will make you sick.

On top of the mesa. Far up the rolling, grassy, tawny plain, in a different life zone, we entered the field of the giant "lilies": the yucca trees—Spanish bayonet (*Yucca arizonica*) and the tall, lovely candles-of-the-desert (*Yucca elata.*) Sometimes mistaken, for a type of cactus, these plants are really members of the lily family. The same is true of the Joshua tree (*Yucca brevifolia*) found far to the west of where I rode that day, in the Mojave desert of Nevada and southeast California. The early Indians had many uses for yucca, fabricating rope, matting, sandals and baskets from the leaf fibers, roasting and eating the fruits and young flower stalks, and making a shampoo from the roots.

Another common plant of the lower deserts, often mistaken for cactus because of its thorny stems, is the ocotillo (*Fouquieria splendens*), also known as flamingsword, candlewood, coachwhip or slimwood. All are good names, aptly descriptive of one part or another of this strange, almost grotesque, but sometimes beautiful shrub. Mature, the ocotillo can reach a height of fifteen feet; it has no trunk but instead a group of flexible, woody, very tough stems branching out from its base on the ground. During the dry season the ocotillo shows nothing much except thorns but let some rain come and within a few days the long stems are clothed in fresh, bright, tiny green leaves, which remain in place for a while, then turn dry and yellowish, falling off as the earth becomes dry again. The high point of the ocotillo's season, however, comes with flowering, when a cluster of brilliant, scarlet flowers blooms at the extreme tip of each nodding branch. Flaming swords. The bees, the hummingbirds, the desert lovers appear from far and wide to sample their rare and startling beauty.

And me and that horse? Nothing unusual. Sometime late in the afternoon Hook and I did part company. Suddenly. Just a little coon-tailed rattlesnake on the trail. I had made the mistake of relaxing for a moment, gazing up at what I thought might be a pair of golden eagles. When the horse bolted he went through the branches of a mesquite tree. I was left behind; it was a long walk home. Hook was watching for me when I got there, looking annoyed because I'd kept him waiting three hours for his dinner. My saddle was still on his back. Good thing for the horse; if he'd lost that saddle I'd have

killed him.

Above. Even a hardy plant like this Joshua tree, near the foothills of the Spring Mountains in the Mojave Desert, celebrates spring with flowers.

First Overleaf. This Teddybear cholla colony is gathered in Pinto Basin, Joshua Tree National Monument, California. Its furry look explains its name, but far from being cuddly and harmless, the Teddybear joints, once lodged in the skin, are difficult and painful to remove.

Second Overleaf. This unusually large elephant tree has a swollen trunk and smooth, scaly, light-colored bark. It is growing on a granite-based alluvial wash in Anza-Borrego State Park, California.

Third Overleaf. A twisted juniper, only partly alive, dominates this view from Green River overlook in Canyonlands National Park, Utah.

144

Above. Mature saguaro cacti such as these in the Superstition Mountains of Arizona may live as long as 200 years and reach a height of 50 feet. This giant cactus has come to symbolize the American desert. Right. A squat hedgehog cactus grows on a granite wall in the Hualapi Mountains of Arizona.

*Below. Saguaro cacti and
ocotillo loom above a ridge in
Altar Valley, Saguaro National
Monument.*

145

*Overleaf. At sunset a colony
of saguaro cacti and ocotillo is
silhouetted against the Quinlan
Mountain Range in Saguaro
National Monument. The
ocotillo's leaves are turning,
and will soon fall off.*

Above. Seemingly invincible to the elements which erode the desert rock and build up the monumental dunes, the saguaro in the Lower Sonoran Desert of Arizona have an air of tranquility as day begins.

Right. A Sonoran Desert sunset creates a blazing backdrop for saguaro cacti along Arizona's Apache Trail.

Overleaf. Along the western base of the Ajo Mountain Drive in Arizona, the organ pipe cacti and saguaro cacti stand tall against the horizon. Unlike its single-trunked neighbor, the organ pipe cactus grows from a base of many stems.

Left. A yucca plant stands out on a stark tableland at White Sands National Monument, New Mexico.
Above. These yuccas, glowing in the light of sunset, seem to float in space at White Sands National Monument.
Overleaf. The "hands" of the cardón cacti reach toward an evening sky in the Vizcaino Desert of Baja California.

Pedestal log fragments from trees 160 million years old were buried under layers of volcanic ash in Petrified Forest National Park, Arizona. The color variations come from mineral solutions of iron and manganese that penetrated the logs.

In the dismal cold and bitter spring of the high desert plateau, once upon a time, I took a job as entrance-station ranger at Petrified Forest National Park. My obligation was to spend eight hours a day in a little cabin at the entrance to the park and sell admission tickets to the tourists coming in off the highway. That was half of it; I also stopped and checked out each car leaving the Park. Looking the driver in the eye, I would say, "Sir, do you have any petrified wood in your car?" The driver would look me back straight in the eye, sincere and honest as only an American can be, and reply, "No sir, we don't." One of the kids in the back seat would say, "But Daddy, what about that big log we put in the trunk?"

I'd have the man open his trunk, remove the stolen petrified log and stack it with other recovered contraband by the station wall. I'd write him a citation that would probably end up costing him $50 or $100, depending on the mood of the local justice of the peace. You couldn't entirely blame the tourist for trying to steal the "wood": it can be sold to any curio dealer for much more than the amount of the fine. If the rangers let them, tourists would soon remove every trace of petrified wood, including the ten-ton giant logs, from their own national park.

That was a bad job. I quit after six weeks and took off for the Grand Canyon, where I spent the sweetest years of my life as a river rat and summertime fire lookout. But the time at Petrified Forest was not a waste. During my off hours in the evening and on weekends I wandered over much of that bleak, beautiful place, under the immaculate Arizona sky, seeking out hidden pockets of wonder, silence, secret animal lives.

Like others, I suppose, when I first heard of petrified wood I imagined a forest of standing trees equipped with limbs, branches, stems, twigs, and leaves, all of it turned to rigid stone. A haunting notion. Perhaps there is such a forest on some other planet, a stone forest with birds of onyx, tourmaline and feldspar perched on brittle branches of agatized rainbow, mineralized chlorophyll, with calcified limbs and silicified trunks. And a stone woodman resting on a stony stump. There must be such a place. One of our children, some-day, will discover it.

Meanwhile, though, we accept the fact that the Petrified Forest is only a graveyard of fallen pine trees, buried for a few million years under

Petrified Wood

various formations of mud and minerals, then finally unburied and exposed—though not *resurrected*—by the shifting worlds of time and change. What actually happened to those logs during their long period of burial?

They were infiltrated and replaced. Buried quickly under mud before the onset of decay, the logs—sometimes with a branch still attached —were penetrated by solutions of such minerals as calcite, silica, pyrite, marcasite, barite, flourite, galena, hematite and sulfur, and sometimes by metals like iron, manganese, uranium. Cell by cell, the circulating minerals replaced the fibrous woody material, preserving exactly the form and structure of the original. Drying and hardening through the centuries, the mass became rock—but rock duplicating every structural detail of the fallen log. Where the log was replaced by certain varieties of minerals and metals, the result is the varicolored beauty of the petrified wood found in Petrified Forest National Park. Rainbows of color, fixed in stone.

Petrified wood can be found in many places in the Southwest deserts. Petrified Forest National Park contains the richest deposit, the most colorful, gemlike, and therefore most valuable lode that we know of. The Park, however, does not contain the biggest intact logs. At several places in the Colorado River drainages, in Utah and Arizona, there are petrified logs, still half buried, that are longer than any to be seen at the Park. The ones I have discovered were mostly gray or black or yellowish, not colorful enough to be considered of gemstone quality. There is a peculiar thrill, however, in stumbling unexpectedly upon one of these long-ago buried but recently exposed fossil monsters. The encounter brings you into direct confrontation with geologic time, with the immensity of the ages, with the mysteries of ancient life; the past becomes real with a sudden, shocking tangibility. There before you, under your fingertips, lies a page out of the story of creation.

Above. Fossilized log fragments, or petrified wood, lie
partially buried in clay at Blue
Mesa in the Petrified Forest.

Overleaf. In the Long Logs
section of the forest are some
of the most strikingly colored
fossilized tree fragments.

*Left. A close-up view of
cemented wood pieces shows
the completeness of metamor-
phosis, the wood being
replaced cell by cell by a
variety of mineral elements.
Below. This cross-sectional
view of a longer log unearthed
from the silt shows the color
variations in the different
layers.*

163

*Overleaf. In the Long Logs
section of the forest, petrified
wood is strewn about in
random chips, lying just about
where it fell millions of
years ago.*

166

The hardy prickly pear of Detrital Valley, Arizona, adapts equally well to freezing snow and desert sun.

Snow on the red rock of Sedona, snow on the gray-blue shales of the Book Cliffs, snow on the crest of the Panamint Mountains seen from the heat and stillness of Badwater Pool ten thousand feet below. Snow on the branches of yucca, on the grotesque limbs of the Joshua trees, and snow crowning the redrock monuments of Castle Valley, Utah. Every brief and fragile crystal is a glittering jewel in its own right, transient but perfect. Blue shadows lie across the snow. And the meaning of the snow: life for the thirsty grass. Life for the animals that feed on the grass. Life for us who live here. The miracle and marvel of snow in the desert.

We had a snowfall the other day. First a blast of wind from the north that continued for an hour, filling the air with dust and cottonwood leaves. Then the snow, falling thickly, softly, quietly, at an angle of thirty degrees, for two hours. The storm stopped all at once, as is the fashion out here in the canyon country. The wind died, the clouds scudded away, the southern sun came out. From turmoil to silent deluge to a blazing, golden, glittering white peace in the span of three hours.

After more than thirty years in the Southwest I am still not entirely adapted to these sudden, shocking changes in the weather. I love them but can never take them entirely for granted, as the natural course of such things. The Southwest desert, with the erratic violence and unpredictability of its storms, is a wonder to me. Usually an exhilarating wonder—but not always.

One November afternoon my rancher and novelist friend William Eastlake and I went out to look for some of his missing cows. This was in the upland, complicated, sagebrush and forest country of northwest New Mexico. He rode off in one direction, I in another. The plan was to circle around and meet on the other side of the mesa. The ride began nicely, with pinyon jays and juncos yawping in the piney woods, the sun in its place. An hour after we separated, however, the sky had become overcast and a north wind was blowing. An hour later I was riding into a blizzard and utterly disoriented, completely lost. I could barely see the horse's ears.

Forgetting the cows, I gave my mount—a little bay mare—free rein, letting her head for the ranch house and home. This horse had been living on Eastlake's ranch, at his expense, for six years—most of its

Desert Snow

life. Panicked by the blinding snow, the mare wanted to run; I let her run. The sooner we got back to shelter the better I'd like it too. We dodged down a vague trail winding through the sagebrush, into the woods. I could see the trees, dim figures through a curtain of fat snowflakes blowing in my eyes. The mare galloped on; I restrained her only enough to remind her I was there.

Nothing looked right. I lost confidence in that horse, pulled her to a stop. Steaming, gulping huge drafts of air, ears twitching, she stared into the white darkness before us. Nothing but falling snow, the trees like apparitions. I could not remember coming through this way; wasn't there a fence, a gate, somewhere about here? Panicking a little myself, I turned the horse and started her back the way we had come. She obeyed without hesitation and when I slacked off on the reins, she began to run again—eagerly, desperately, exactly as she had done in the opposite direction.

So much for the homing sense of that four-legged fool; we were both lost. I yanked her round again, dismounted, led her on foot off the trail through the deepening snow toward an overhanging cliff I could barely see on our right. I tied the horse to a tree and tried to get a fire started with wet wood. This was not going to be easy. After many matches, I coaxed some shavings into flame and made a fire. The snow stopped falling, the wind died, the stars appeared, and I heard a rifle going off, three quick shots, not far away. Eastlake was out looking for me, much more worried, by that time, than I was. We were only a couple of miles from his house after all.

An hour later we were sitting in front of a roaring stove, drinking hot buttered rum and telling lies, happy to be alive.

169

Above. On an evening in February a twisted Joshua tree and cholla cactus are laden with mountain snow—the leftovers of a storm that swept over the northern slope of the San Gabriel Mountains in the Mojave Desert.

First Overleaf. A lacy pattern of plant stalks decorates snowy drifts in January along the Colorado River near Moab, Utah.

Second Overleaf. Solid outlines of Joshua plants and granite outcroppings stand out during a mild snowstorm in the Jumbo Rocks section of Joshua Tree National Monument, California.

Third Overleaf. Light February snows on the limestone and shale formations of the Goosenecks of the San Juan River/Honaker Trail, near Mexican Hat, Utah.

Fourth Overleaf. Blackbrush and sage are covered with luminous snow crystals in Utah's Virgin River Valley.

Fifth Overleaf. Snowdrifts—unusually heavy for this area—surround patches of soap tree yucca, saltbrush, and rabbit brush scattered on a gypsum dune at White Sands National Monument, New Mexico.

Alkali salt formations are clustered near ancient springs at the bottom of Death Valley in California.

Noon on the alkali flats, Death Valley, California. Early September.
Not the best of times to be here but necessary. Necessary because
I've never done it before and I have to find out what it's like.
Still summertime in Death Valley. Here the summer lasts from April
to December. There is hardly a winter at all, although its forms
of passage can be seen on the mountains above the valley. Telescope
Peak, the highest point near by, rises 11,045 feet above the
valley floor at Badwater, which, at 282 feet below sea level, is the
lowest point.
My pickup truck is parked by the road, ready for a quick getaway.
I hope. The motor is shut off. If it won't start this time my best bet
would be to spend the afternoon under the truck. That would be the
only shade within ten miles of here. I've got my hat on and a full
canteen of water in the cab, but Death Valley is no place for a long
hike by day at this time of year.
The point is to sit quietly, or lie quietly, in the shade, and listen. And
suffer, a little, if you feel it worth your time.
This part of the valley is perfectly still. The silence is absolute. Or
nearly so. I can feel and almost hear the beating of my heart. For a
moment I imagine that I hear the sound that a few clouds are making
as they pass above the distant mountains. But that couldn't be
happening; I am only wishing that I could hear them.
Silence. The sound of nothing. There's a lot of that around here. The
desert is clear. And clean. And terrifyingly simple. A man could go
stark raving mad, naked under the sun, with all these square miles
of simplicity.
I peer out from the shade of my hat brim into the white glare of
the salt flats. Close by is a wilderness of jagged, cutting, nearly
impenetrable salt formations, knee-high blades and swords and
stalagmites built up over the years by capillary action. Walking
a half mile over and through that crackling, crusted, ulcerous
terrain would be a laborious project. A labor of love. Little pools of
briny water lie here and there among dust-stained pinnacles.
Farther out the spiny crust seems to disappear. In the distance—
miles away—the salt flats appear smooth as ice. White and smooth.
At other places on other salt flats men have driven land vehicles
at four hundred and fifty miles an hour. Maybe faster. We don't
know what the possible limit is.

Saltscapes

But I do hear it. A ticking sound; the only sound amidst nothing. Something is stirring out there, out here, all around me. I kneel close to the nearest pillar of salt, bending an ear. The noise is made by expansion. The day is still heating up—it's only 115°F. here at the moment, according to the thermometer in the shade of my truck— and salt crusts are expanding under the sun. Minute particles of alkali flake off, slide into the clear pool.

The water too is active, or reactive, evaporating into the air, leaving behind more salt.

This is one of my favorite places in the world. After I die I'm coming back here—for a while. For an eon or two. As a spirit, of course, not as a creature of flesh and blood and bone and fear. There are some living things in this awful wasteland of salt and emptiness. There is a species of tiny shrimp in some of the briny pools close by, including Badwater Pool itself. Together with the various micro-organisms on which the little shrimp survive. But on the whole, this is not a good place for any larger animals, least of all for man. The vulture's shadow—but little else—passes across these pinnacles of salt, crusted with wind-blown dust and sand. And the vulture passes only to reach less barren ground beyond.

Standing here, looking at and listening to the immensity of space and time, I think of the English explorer, Robert Falcon Scott. Lost in the Antarctic with all of his men, back in 1912, dying in an endless white night of wind, snow and ice, Scott wrote these last words in his diary: "Great God, this is a terrible place."

Down in Death Valley on a clear, still, sunlit day. In the sinkhole of the western hemisphere. Gathering storm clouds hang above the distant mountains, promising the miracle of rain, but where I stand the sun blazes down through preternatural silence. Alone on the floor of the great American desert.

183

Above. When the waters of Lake Manley evaporated, only thin towers of salt remained at the "Devil's Golf Course" in Death Valley. In the distance to the left lie the Black Mountains.

Overleaf. A storm lingering over the distant Panamint Range throws the salt deposits on the "Devil's Golf Course" into sharp relief. Vegetation is sparse and the soil is briny and inhospitable toward budding plant life.

186

Above. Algae interacting with freshwater springs at California's Mono Lake cause unique calcium formations in this region of the Sierra Nevadas. The lake waters are slowly receding.
Right. One of the few plants that can survive in the briny, alkaline soil of Death Valley's Salt Creek is the pickleweed, which has a large tolerance for alkali salt.

187

Above. Formations of volcanic tufa rise above briny Pyramid Lake in Nevada.

Overleaf. Saltbushes, stout shrubs partial to alkaline soils, flourish in Death Valley. The Mesquite Flat dunes are on the skyline, and the Cotton-wood Mountains are to the northwest.

Summer rain begins to moisten
the cracked, dry mudflats
below Book Cliffs in southern
Utah.

Dry lakes are common in the Southwestern desert. Where rainfall is low and the topography mountainous, it happens often that surface water never gets to a river, never reaches the sea. Some of our *rivers* never reach the sea. The Amargosa in California, the Truckee and Humboldt in Nevada, the Sevier in Utah, for example. Not that any of these are much like real rivers. In most parts of the nation they would barely qualify as creeks. But they are permanent, they do flow—or did before the white man began fooling around with them.

Where intermittent water flows into a landlocked basin, it evaporates, leaving behind what the Spanish call a *playa*, what we call a dry lake. Since the streams that feed these basins carry a heavy salt content from the surrounding hills, the dry lakes are generally too saline for much plant life. You will see shad scale or saltbush, arrowweed, pickleweed, tamarisk, horsetails—salt-tolerant plants—but not much else.

In the basin and range country of Nevada, Utah, Arizona, West Texas, southeast California and eastern Oregon you find dry lake beds between every pair of mountain ranges. Like any recent water-deposited formation, the dried and alkaline mud of these lakes is perfectly level, flat as a pool table. Seen from far off, they resemble fields of snow, lenses of sugar. The heat waves build up thickly here, transforming the purple mountains beyond into floating ships on a sea of gin. Hawks and vultures drift into the air above the dry lakes, catch rising thermal columns and soar far up into the blue. During the day no other life appears. At night the rodents come out from the desert scrub with the rabbits and snakes and scorpions and tarantulas, leaving long meandering trails across the mud. The coyotes watch, yipping and hollering.

After a flood, after the water has vanished into the hot sky, the mud begins to dry and shrink. Shrinking, it cracks, leaving deep narrow crevasses; the crust curls up at the edges, forming plates, saucers, cakes and scallops of baked, ceramic mud that you can pick up and spin through the air like Frisbees. They crunch and clatter like a field of cornflakes when you walk across them.

At a desolate and lonely playa in Death Valley called the Race Track, some rocks have made their way down from the surrounding slopes and begun a slow, intermittent slide across the dry lake bed. All

191

Mud Mosaics

move—when they move—in the same direction; the trails they leave on the mud are precisely parallel. Their progress is slow, their moments of actual motion rare. At the rate they are moving it will take them a century or more to cross the flat. I don't know of anyone who claims to have seen these rocks in motion but there is a plausible explanation: after a rain, when the clayish surface of the lake bed is slick and greasy, a wind may come up strong enough to push the rocks a few inches forward. The advance of the rocks is parallel because, according to this theory, the wind here always blows from the same direction. To confirm this theory by observation you would have to go there, after a good rain in the area, and wait for a very strong wind to come before the mud is dried. The difficulty with this test is that it seldom rains anywhere in Death Valley, and even when it does the rain is usually preceded, not followed, by strong winds.

My theory is that there are some Indians living up in the hills, remnants of the ancient Goshute tribe never seen by whites, and that they come down to the valley now and then, when they feel like it, and simply push those rocks forward by hand. Or by magic. Their purpose, I believe, is to confuse us. When we have become sufficiently confused, the Goshutes think, we whites will go back to Ohio or Connecticut or Europe or wherever we came from. Since this rock-pushing has been going on for many, many decades the Goshutes must be a patient people. Patient, persistent, and hopeful. I admire those qualities but think they are mistaken. They should come out of hiding and join us. The white folks will not go away. We are all in this valley together now.

193

A dry lake bed, or playa, near Baker, Nevada is barren of vegetation. The Snake Range is faintly visible in the background.

Below. Evaporating water leaves behind a large mosaic of dried alkali cakes on the flats in Death Valley.
Right. The playa at the Race Track in Death Valley is a mass of oozing, slippery mud after a heavy cloudburst, but it soon dries out and hardens.

First Overleaf. Dried alkali cakes form an elaborate pattern in the shadow of Tucki Mountain in Death Valley. Flash floods alter these patterns.
Second Overleaf. A close-up view of salt tiles dried by the sun into an intricate web design at Dumont dunes in the Mojave Desert.

200

Representing the classic period of the Anasazi pueblo, Long House ruin stretches across the base of Wetherill Mesa, in Mesa Verde National Park, Colorado.

Betatakin is surely one of the most fantastic little cities on earth. The archetypal cliff dwelling, it sits perched like a cluster of swallows' nests high in a grotto in the face of a 500-foot cliff. Built about nine hundred years ago, then suddenly and mysteriously abandoned. At least we think it was a sudden departure. Numerous artifacts were left behind—pottery, sandals, baskets, arrow points, coral and turquoise jewelry, even ears of corn.

Betatakin and its neighboring town, Keet Seel, dramatic as they appear even today, were not the largest or greatest cliff dwellings. The Anasazi (Navajo for "the old ones") created their finest work in what is now Mesa Verde National Park.

The story of the discovery of these magnificent ruins begins on a snowy day in December 1888. Two cowboys were riding the rim of the mesa, searching for strayed cattle. One was Richard Wetherill, the other Charlie Mason. Riding through the forest of pinyon pine and juniper that covers most of the mesa, they reached a clearing on the edge of a canyon. At once they saw it: under a deep, overhanging alcove in the opposite canyon wall, facing the south (as all cliff dwellings do), was a small city of stone, silent and empty. Within the shallow cave formed by the alcove was a tower four stories high, surrounded by dozens of smaller structures. Wetherill and Mason, unable to descend into the precipitous canyon, rode far around to the head of it, found a way down, fought their way through brush and rocks, and reached the long abandoned town. Exploring the ruins—200 rooms, 23 kivas or ceremonial chambers— they picked up corncobs, pottery, stone tools; a few human skeletons were lying about; wood rats scurried through the debris-filled storage rooms. They named the ruin Cliff Palace—a romantic but less than accurate designation, for this pueblo was not a palace but a former town which could have accommodated four hundred inhabitants. Exploring farther to the west, Wetherill and Mason discovered a second ghostly town, not so large as Cliff Palace but better preserved; this one—114 rooms, 8 kivas—is now called Spruce Tree House. The next day they came upon a third—Balcony House. All three are now among the most popular and heavily visited archaeological sites in the national park system.

News of the cowboys' discovery was not long in getting about. One early visitor was an F. H. Chapin, who came in 1890, recording the

Cliff Dwellings

visit in his diary: "We remained long and ransacked the structure from one end to another." Cliff-dweller artifacts were then, as they are now, highly negotiable merchandise. The Wetherills sold their first collection of pots, arrow points, stone tools, skeletons, for $3,000—a handsome sum in 1889.

Another visitor was Baron Gustav Nordenskiold, amateur archaeologist from Sweden. His initial impression of Cliff Palace is worth quoting:

"With its round towers and high walls rising out of heaps of stones deep in the mysterious twilight of the cavern, and defying in their sheltered site the ravages of time, Cliff Palace resembles at a distance an enchanted castle." He too carried off an extensive load of souvenirs, now to be seen in a museum in Finland! Nordenskiold also commented on the odd T-shaped doorways, wide at the upper end, narrow at the lower. No one has given a final explanation of this architectural curiosity. He was also impressed by the masonry: "The stones are carefully dressed and laid in regular courses: the walls are perpendicular, sometimes leaning slightly inwards at the same angle all around the room—this being part of the design. The corners form almost perfect right angles . . ."

Nothing could seem more solid and permanent than this stone architecture; yet the people of Mesa Verde abandoned their homes at various times during the years A.D. 1200 to 1300. By the end of the century all had become ghost towns.

From the many canyons of Utah, northern Arizona, and southwestern Colorado, this mass migration took place at about the same time in the 13th century. Hundreds of painstakingly constructed villages and towns, none with quite so spectacular a setting as Betatakin and Keet Seel but some much larger, were left behind during this time. Thousands of people set out on foot—they had no domestic animals but dogs—and headed south toward the river valleys of New Mexico and Arizona. That which they could they carried on their backs—or on their heads. Although the present-day Pueblo Indians, the Zuñis, the Hopis, are probably descendants of the ancient cliff dwellers, they kept no historical records and apparently have no tribal memory (other than a few vague legends) of that vast movement southward seven hundred years ago. And that

is one of the strangest things of all. How could so great an event, taking place barely yesterday in the time-scale of human history, have left no memory in the minds, legends, and myths of the modern tribesmen who are the inheritors of that tradition?

Why did the cliff dwellers give up their homes? Many hypotheses have been proposed. Marauding enemy tribes. Inter-clan feuding. Plagues and epidemics. Crop failures due to a prolonged drought that took place at the time, as can be verified through the study of tree-ring cycles. Possibly some mystical or religious event, a sudden fear of a disaster even greater than uprooting and migration. Meteors in the night sky, omens and portents. Or something so prosaic as exhaustion of the soil.

The cliff dwellers were farmers. We believe that they built their villages up in canyon walls for purposes of defense; evidently they lived in great fear of attack. But they could not make a living in an alcove in a sandstone wall, let alone find sufficient water there. Therefore they farmed the bottomlands, raising maize, beans, squash, melons, chili, just as the Hopis and Pueblo people do today. The crops were harvested and stored in the little huts of stone and adobe, roofed with juniper, that were built in a safer place above. Undoubtedly these vegetarian foods were supplemented by game, when available—deer, rabbit, porcupine, birds, an occasional bighorn sheep. In all probability the people slaughtered and cooked their domesticated dogs when a *pièce de résistance* was required for the menu, as on feast days, holy days, or for the delectation of visiting dignitaries.

We are tempted to smile at the naive customs of the paleolithics. But they might laugh at ours. Our one clear point of superiority is that we study them rather than the other way around. But as some have suggested, the time will come when we too are objects of another culture's investigations, when our ruins are measured and our garbage dumps sifted, weighed, analyzed.

The cliff dwellers were a stone-age people. They had no metals. Their weapons and tools were made of stone and wood; they made fire with hand drills. To reach their airy homes, many of which are now inaccessible, they chipped finger and toe holds in the sandstone cliffs, and made ladders, the rungs inset in notches in the upright poles and bound in place with yucca fibers or animal sinews. They fought their enemies and hunted game with bows and arrows and perhaps also with lances and spears; many large flint points, probably spearheads, have been found. (Years ago a fellow ranger and I were exploring a canyon in what is now Arches National Park. I stepped right over a three-inch, elegantly chipped spearhead; the fellow behind me found it. I'd been looking ahead at the sky and landscape; he kept his eyes on the ground, watching his step. He is now superintendent of an important national park.)

Visiting one of the famous cliff dwellings today, Betatakin say, or Keet Seel, or the grand constructions of Mesa Verde and Chaco Canyon, and looking at those cold, empty, half-ruined stone remains, we might think that life there must have been a hard, tiresome and precarious business. But don't be too quick to think so. The evidence shows that these people had plenty of time for art, ceremony, religion. Like stone-age people known today, most of them probably spent no more than two or three days a week in actual subsistence labor. The women ground corn with mano and metate, a tedious task, as it would seem. (The mano a hand-held stone, the metate a stone bowl—like pestle and mortar.) But they sat together in groups to do their work and we can imagine, from what we know of Indians today, that they passed the time in gossip, storytelling, songs and laughter. Furthermore the work they did was dignified by necessity, and therefore of high value.

Meanwhile the men, heavy with their solemnity and manly responsibilities, avoided the routine chores by gathering in underground ceremonial rooms—the kivas—to rehearse all-important religious rites (taboo for women), prepare masks and costumes for the next dance, initiate pubescent boys into manhood, and also—no doubt—indulge in games, the neolithic version of poker, maybe, with a little serious drinking and an occasional stag party thrown in for fun.

Above. "T"-shaped doorways such as this one at Mesa Verde's Mug House ruin have long mystified scholars. It is thought that they had a spiritual as well as practical significance.

Overleaf. On a similar snowy day, almost a century ago, Mesa Verde was discovered by two cowboys trailing stray cattle. This site is called Square House Tower.

Left. Another view of Long House among the Anasazi ruins reveals its intricate design.
Right Above. The kiva, or ceremonial chamber, at the Mug House ruin.
Right Below. The Spring House ruin at Mesa Verde will not be excavated until more advanced techniques for archeological study are developed.
Overleaf. Rainwashed cliffs tower above Keet Seel ruin in Navajo National Monument, Arizona.

208

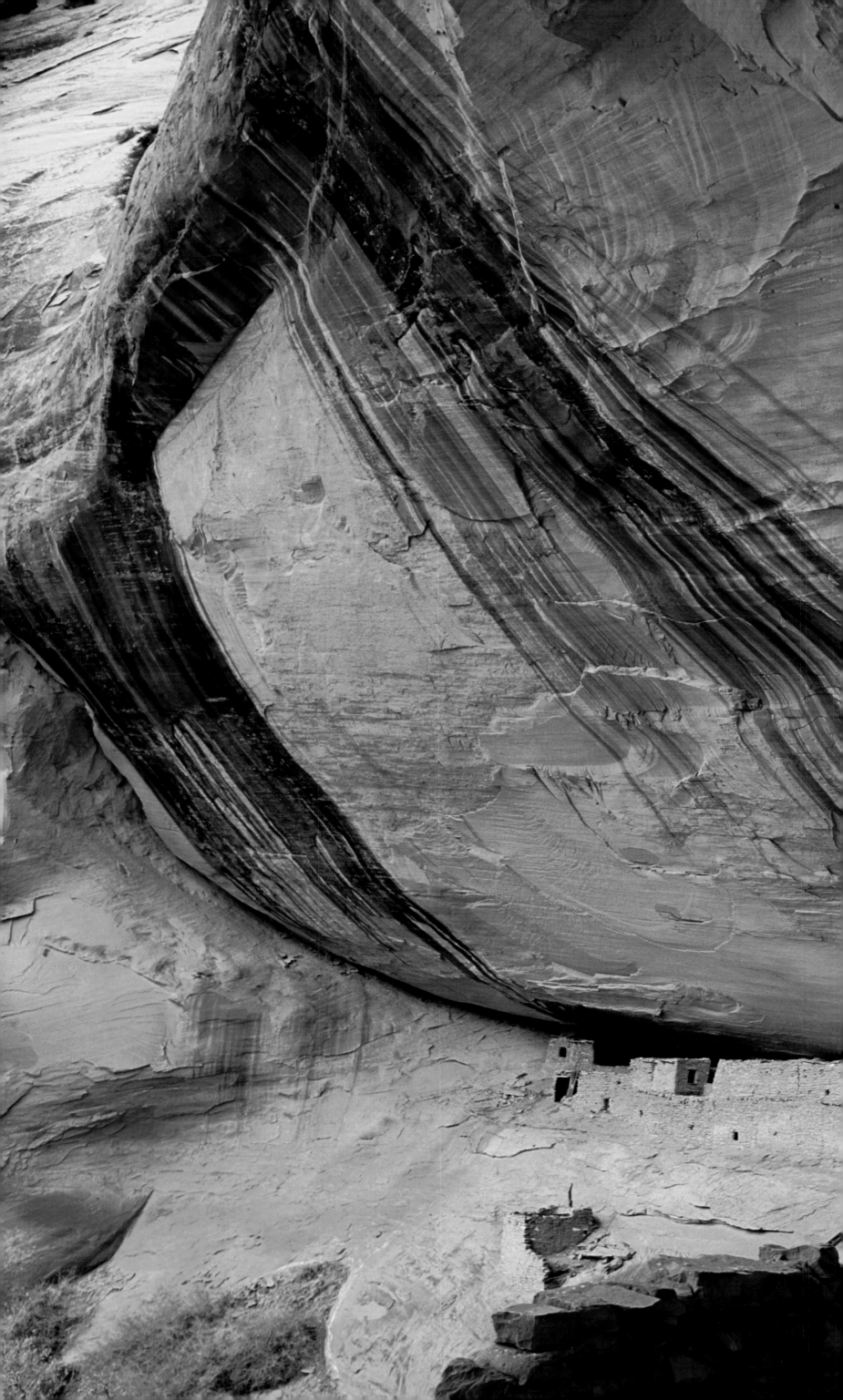

*Above. A kiva and ruined
walls at Keet Seel, Navajo
National Monument.
Left. Taking advantage of the
natural rock shelter, this cliff
dwelling was built directly
under an enormous rainwashed
sandstone cliff at Keet Seel.
Overleaf. Influenced by the
success of the Anasazi, other
desert peoples built similar
pueblos, such as this one at
Gila Cliff Dwellings National
Monument in New Mexico,
secure from enemy attack and
with a commanding view of the
surrounding terrain.*

Below. A lone prehistoric cliff dwelling at Gila National Monument is inaccessible except by means of shallow finger and toe holds carved out of the rock, or by primitive ladders.

Right Above. An abandoned mission church and a kiva at Pecos National Monument, New Mexico, stand at opposite ends of a 900-year span. Right Below. The large block wall at Chettro Kettle in Chaco Canyon National Monument, New Mexico, was constructed by such skilled craftsmen that it still remains in excellent condition.

216

Overleaf. *Acoma Pueblo in
New Mexico, still inhabited, is
a living link, across a span
of seven centuries, to the
Anasazi way of life.*

217

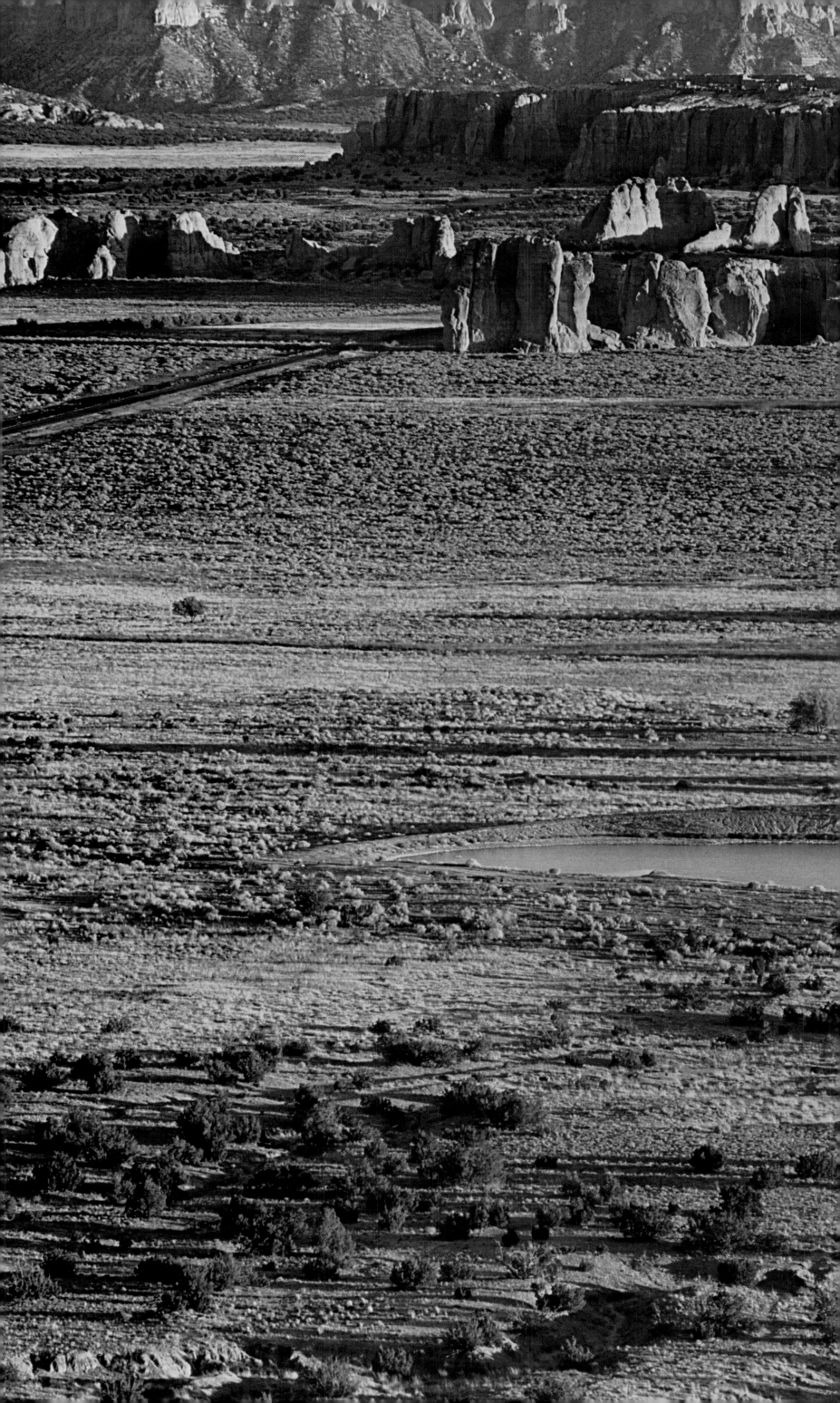

This bighorn sheep petroglyph was pecked in sandstone varnish at Salt Creek in Arches National Park, Utah.

Everywhere you go in the Southwestern deserts you come across drawings on the rocks, on the canyon walls. Some are inscribed into the rock—petroglyphs. Some are painted on the rock—pictographs. All of them, pictographs and petroglyphs alike, present an odd and so far untranslated language. If it is a language.

Not that the pictures are always hard to understand. Most consist of recognizable figures: deer, bighorn sheep, antelope, sometimes a mastodon (extinct no more than 10,000 years in North America), serpents, centipedes, rain clouds, the sun, dancing humans, warriors with shields and lances, even men on horseback—representations which cannot be more than four hundred years old, when the Spaniards introduced the horse to North America.

Some of the pictures, however, are disturbingly strange. We see semihuman figures with huge blank eyes, horned heads. Ghostly shapes resembling men but without feet or legs float on the air. Human-like forms with helmets and goggles wave tentacles at us: what can they be? Gods? Goddesses? Cosmonauts from the Betelgeuse neighborhood? Here's a fighter with shield painted red, white and blue—the all-American man. And still other forms appear, completely nonrepresentational, totally abstract symbols of— of what? Nobody knows. The American Indians of today, if they know, aren't telling. Probably they are as mystified by them as we are. Preoccupied with reproduction, multiplication and getting ahead, the Indians of today have little interest in a frivolous hobby: the study of desert rock art. In any case the culture of the modern native Americans has little connection with the culture of the vanished rock artists. The continuity was broken long ago.

What does the rock art mean? Unlike the story of the cliff ruins, fairly coherent to archaeologists, we know little of the significance of this ancient work. Perhaps it was only doodling of a sort. A bunch of stone-age deer hunters sit in camp day after day with nothing to do (the game is gone), telling lies, chipping arrowheads, straightening arrow shafts with their doughnut-like straightener stones. One of them, wanting to record his lies for posterity, begins to incise the image of a six-point buck on the overhanging cliff wall. I killed that animal, he boasts, with my own hands. Another liar takes up the challenge. I killed six bighorn rams, he claims, in this very canyon, only fourteen years ago. And he tallies

Images on Rock

the total on the soft sandstone with a hard-edged chunk of agate or basalt or flint.

These shallow scratchings may have been the beginning. Inevitably the power of art took over. Most hunter-warriors were artists. They had to be. They made their own weapons. A weapon, to be useful, has to be well made. A well-made weapon or any well-made tool, when crafted by hand, can be considered a work of art.

Perhaps the rock art was created by specialists. By shamans and wizards, evoking sympathetic magic to aid the hunt. Portraying a deer slain by an arrow, the medicine man would believe that his wishes would serve as efficient cause in producing the desired result. Imitative magic: life imitates art. Thus the pictographs and petroglyphs may have had a religious denotation, hunting being central to any hunter's religion.

The art served as a record. As practical magic. And as communication between wanderers. Water around the next bend, a certain zigzag sign might mean. We killed eleven bighorn here, only two hundred years ago, says a second. *We were here, say the hunters. We were here, say the artists.*

What about the spectral forms, the ghosts, ghouls, gods? Supernatural beings are fished from dreams. From the caves of Altamira to the base of Ayers Rock in central Australia, all original, aboriginal people have believed in the power of dreams. In the Dream Time, say the wise old men of the outback, we made our beginning; from the Dream Time we come; into the Dream Time, after death, we shall return. The dream is the real; waking life is only a dream within a greater dream.

These are speculations. Only a few anthropologists, like New Mexico's Dr. Polly Schaafsma, have given the Indian rock art serious attention. Most have observed the drawings, recorded them, but made no further study. At this time there is no method known by which the pictographs and petroglyphs can be dated accurately; dendrochronology (tree rings) and the carbon-14 technique cannot be applied here. Nor can the art be correlated with other archaeological data—cliff dwellings, burial sites, the various styles of pottery-, basket-, and tool-making. In the absence of verifiable scientific information the interpretation of rock art has been left
222 by default to popular fancy: thus the early and premature labeling

of this art as a form of "writing" or "hieroglyphs." Not surprising.
The first reaction of anyone seeing these strange pictures for the
first time is the naturally human: what do they *mean*?

Perhaps we will never learn what, if anything, this kind of art
"means." Meaning is not of primary importance here. What is important is the recognition of art, wherever we may discover it, in
whatever form. These canyon paintings and canyon inscriptions
are valuable for their own sake, as work of elegance, freshness,
originality (in the original sense of the word), economy of line,
precision of point, integrity of materials. They are beautiful. And
all of them hundreds of years old—some may be much, much older.
An art exposed to the elements and the vandalism of our con-
temporaries; some of my neighbors like to use them for target
practice and some scribble over them with spray paint the ineffably
insignificant signatures of their own transient and debased existence. Understandable—but regrettable. Dots, lines, spirals, zigzags,
undulations, circles. The last mentioned, especially, seem to attract
rifle bullets. A serious mistake. Let the old shaman Black Elk speak
on this matter: "Behold the circle of the nation's hope, for it is holy,
being endless. Thus all power shall be one power in the people
without end."

The artist Paul Klee, whose surreal work much resembles some of
this desert rock art, wrote in his *Diaries 1898-1918:* "There are
two mountains on which the weather is bright and clear, the
mountain of the animals and the mountain of the gods. But between
lies the shadowy valley of men."

A literal interpretation of the rock art might be interesting, even
useful, for understanding of the culture of these anonymous hunter-
artists. But it is not at all necessary for the enjoyment of what
they made. The aesthetic appeal of this art is stronger than any
possible translation we might make of it. Art for the sake of art,
in this case at least, may be all we will ever have. Looking at those
godlike figures on the wall, those haunting symbols whose key is
lost, we cannot help but feel that the persons who made them were
engaged in something deeper than the urge to decorate. They were
communicating to one another, if not to us, a configuration of ideas
and emotions about their world. Ideas and emotions which cannot be
transliterated into the terms of verbal language.

223

On many walls in the desert we find the figure of the humpbacked flute player, Kokopelli (a Hopi name). A wanderer, for sure, and a man of strange powers, compensating for his deformity. Kokopelli may have been the Pied Piper who led the cliff dwellers out of the canyons, out of their fear, and down to the high, open country to the south, where the people could live more like humans and less like bats. Maybe he was a nomadic witch doctor, a healer of bodies and curer of feverishly imaginative savage souls. Speculations. . . . Nobody knows. The memory of the actual Kokopelli, if he was an actual person, has been lost. Only the outline of Kokopelli, his image chiseled into rock, has survived. Too bad. Many of us would like very much to hear the music that he played.

The American desert was discovered by an unknown people. They tried its deepest secrets. Now they have vanished, extinct as the tapir and the coryphodon. But the undeciphered message that they left us still remains, written on the walls. A message preserved not in mere words and numbers but in the durable images of art. Of a high and lasting art, human, vivid, and powerful.

Still we grope for meanings. What do they mean, these signs and symbols on the rock? What do they say? All forms of art, including the art of poetry, seek to transcend language. Language, in the mind of a poet, seeks to transcend itself. Art edifies, entertains, instructs, records but most important attempts "to grasp the thing which has no name." It seems reasonable to suppose that the unknown people who left this record of their passage felt the same impulse toward permanence, the same longing for communion with the world that we feel today. To ask for any more meaning may be as futile as to ask for a meaning in the desert itself. What does the desert mean? It means what it is. It is there, it will be there when we are gone. But for a while we living things—men, women, birds, coyotes howling far off on yonder stony ridge—we were a part of it all. That should be enough.

225

Above. A scorpion and antelope design on the desert wall, found in the Colorado River canyon in southern Utah, is still legible.

First Overleaf. This complex petroglyph found in 9-Mile Canyon in central Utah may represent the ancient peoples' belief that hunting and magic were closely entwined. Second Overleaf. Another example of symbolic rock art in 9-Mile Canyon, remarkably well preserved.

*Below. The figures on these
shields suggest that plainsmen
and pueblo peoples of the
Galisteo Basin, New Mexico,
were acquainted with each
other.
Right. The mythical Kokopelli,
a humpbacked flute player, is
depicted on volcanic rock in
Galisteo Basin.*

230

*First Overleaf. This mysterious
petroglyph is etched on sandstone in Valley of Fire State
Park, Nevada.
Second Overleaf. A close-up of
the legendary Kokopelli with
his shield, carved on volcanic
rock in Galisteo Basin.*

The Photographer

David Muench's commitment to photographing the desert's many faces began in his boyhood. Growing up in California, he was fascinated by the desert and soon started an album of pictures of it. Later, he attended several universities and then studied photography at the Art Center in Los Angeles. He specializes in photographing nature, especially Western landscapes, all the while returning to the desert to record its haunting beauty and also its harsher aspects. He adds that he still needs these regular photographic odysseys in the desert as a counterpoint to his other work. Most of the lyrical and impressionistic yet wonderfully explicit images were made in the last three years.

David Muench's other books include California *(with Ray Atkeson),* Arizona *and* Timberline Ancients. *Recently he was commissioned by the U.S. Parks Service to photograph thirty-three large murals depicting the Lewis and Clark Trail; these murals are permanently displayed in the Jefferson Expansion Memorial, St. Louis's "Gateway to the West."*

The Author

Edward Abbey is a well-known novelist, a maverick conservationist, and a sometime park ranger. "If a label is required," he once said with characteristic bluntness, "say that I am one who loves unfenced country." *Mr. Abbey's loyalties are fierce. As expressed in his writings, he feels deep affection for natural wilderness areas and is outraged by any encroachment on them by civilization. Many of his books have desert themes, such as his highly regarded novel,* Desert Solitaire. *He is also the author of* Cactus Country, Slick Rock: Endangered Canyons of the Southwest, *the* Monkey Wrench Gang, *the text of* Appalachian Wilderness *(with Eliot Porter's photographs) and* The Journey Home, *a collection of essays in defense of the West. Mr. Abbey lives near the Southwest desert, having moved from his Pennsylvania home thirty years ago. He still spends summers on lonely peaks as a fire warden in the Western wilderness.*

237

Index

Prepared and produced by Chanticleer Press, Inc.
Publisher: Paul Steiner
Editor-in-Chief: Gudrun Buettner
Executive Editor: Susan Costello
Managing Editor: Jane Opper
Project Editor: Susan Rayfield
Production: Helga Lose
Art Director: Carol Nehring

Design: Massimo Vignelli